Victorian Fashions

Volume II
1890-1905

by Hazel Ulseth & Helen Shannon

Edited by Donna H. Felger

Photography by Hazel and Marty Ulseth

Published by Hobby House Press

Cumberland, Maryland 21502

Dedication

To Pat Stall in recognition of her love of dolls, her creativity and her generous contributions which have added so much to the world of doll collectors.

Additional copies of this book may be purchased at $14.95
from
HOBBY HOUSE PRESS, INC.
900 Frederick Street
Cumberland, Maryland 21502
or from your favorite bookstore or dealer.
Please add $1.75 per copy postage.

Printed in the United States of America

ISBN: 0-87588-329-X

Table of Contents

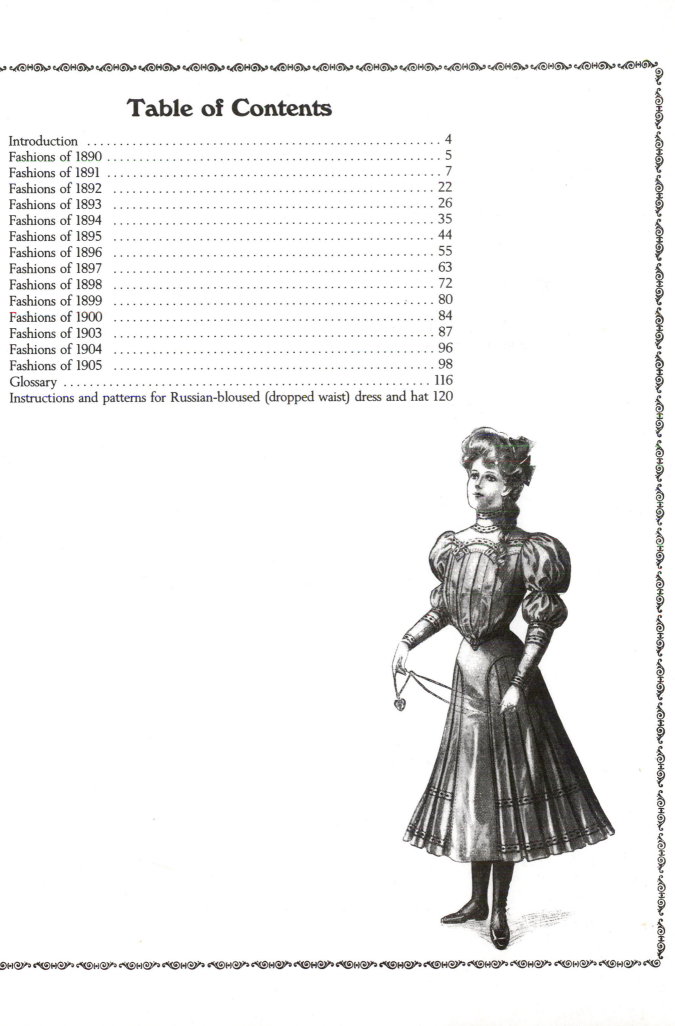

Introduction

This book, the fifth in a series offered by Hobby House Press, Inc., covers Victorian fashions for the period 1890 to 1905, featuring styles for ladies and girls. All five books, which follow a similar format, are listed here showing the fold-out patterns, which are included in each book:

1) *Antique Children's Fashions* with 50 pages of fashion illustrations and a fold-out pattern for a 20½in (52cm) doll dress and hat.

2) *Boys' Fashions*, concentrating on fashions for boys, includes two fold-out patterns, a size 17in (43cm) kilt, cap and boots, and a size 19in (48cm) sailor suit and hat.

3) *Bridal Fashions*, the third in the series, features brides and bridesmaids with a fold-out pattern for a lovely bridal gown and a variation for the bridesmaid, designed to fit a fashion doll of 22½in (57cm). It also includes other related items such as fashions for "mothers of the bride," bridal accessories and hints for the groom and his attendants.

4) *Victorian Fashions I (1870-1890)* features styles for ladies and girls, as shown in more than 100 plates from fashion magazines of the period, and a lovely fold-out pattern. This pattern for a 23in (58cm) doll consists of a charming frock with bouffant skirt banded by wide lace trim, topped by a unique bodice tapered to a point at center front, small mandarin collar and distinctive sleeves with high, lace-covered cuffs and very full upper sleeves. Do not stop at this point! You will also find patterns for an outdoor outfit consisting of a fur-trimmed cloak, bonnet and muff to match.

5) In this volume, *Victorian Fashions II, (1890-1905)* you will be enchanted with two fold-out patterns. The first is for a dropped waist or Russian-bloused dress for a stately 28in (71cm) doll. The same pattern is repeated for a 16½in (42cm) doll, with variations in fabrics and trim. In addition, for the larger size there is a lovely hat constructed on a wired frame, bouncy and chic with its flounce and ribbons.

All five books have many fashion illustrations arranged in chronological order, styles in most cases having been selected from *The Delineator** and from other fashion magazines of the period such as *McCalls* and *Butterick*, thus offering authenticity in the evolution of fashions during this period, as well as in fabrics and colors used, and interesting details about style lines and construction methods.

While these books are designed for doll costumers and doll collectors, the subject matter has a much broader application in the field of costume design. Theatrical costume designers will find invaluable details as they work with period pieces.

Paper doll makers rely heavily on such sources for the styles used in depicting paper dolls dressed in period costumes.

Another important function is served by these books in allowing correct identification of old costumes found in attics and at garage sales, since the purchaser can make comparisons with illustrations from *The Delineator* and label the costume according to the era in which it was made and determine functions for which it was appropriate.

For the fashion buff who tries to trace the trends of fashion from one century to another, the international flavor of styles during this period (1870-1905) offers a variety of surprises. We have talked about the Normandy bonnet before this, and many readers are aware that it appears often in our patterns. However, some of the styles which were obviously borrowed directly from European and Mediterranean history are fascinating. From North Africa we have the burnoose, or loose-hooded cloak used by the Arabs as protection against the burning equatorial sun, and the Zouave jacket taken from the same area. The French Kings Louis XV and Louis XVI contributed from their wardrobes women's jackets fashioned on the same lines, using the broad lapels and wide collars of lavish and beautiful lace. The Killarney cloak obviously has its origin in Ireland, while Scotland lent us its famous tam-o'-shanter, a style that is still with us.

The famous artist who loved to dress his subjects in long flowing robes lent his name later to the Watteau cloak, Spain brought the Toreador jacket to fashion, Moliere lent us his vest, while from Italy came the Garibaldi vest, and once again from France, the Tudor collars. The Grecian influence was more than just popular as it lent traditional garb and the art of "living statues" to parlor entertainment. German influence is seen in the Gretchen dress for children with its Gretchen sleeves. So fashion designers looked for new ideas then, just as our own fashion designers of the 20th century look back for inspiration.

For the amateur fashion buff, the book provides many hours of pleasurable browsing...and a little nostalgia for the "olden days" of our grandmother. For the doll costumer, this material provides an incomparable source of style information for a period in which many dolls were being manufactured, a period which in fact provides us with great diversification of doll production which has become the mainstay of doll collectors today, our wonderful German and French bisques.

Many dolls were dressed at the factories or through home industries, but many arrived at their new homes clad only in crude cotton chemises, so had to depend on their new owners for proper styling.

With the passage of years and several generations, many dolls need to be re-dressed and in this field we hope to offer the doll costumers a wide variety of styles and suggestions for kind, color and texture of fabrics...all properly orchestrated to make a treasured doll a "thing of beauty and a joy forever."

So here you should find all the stimuli necessary to whet your appetites for costuming a doll, either using patterns available and with your own imaginations creating a unique but authentic costume by using the illustrations to draft original patterns. We hope you have discovered the first books to be useful and inspiring and that this, the fifth book, will not only be a welcome and useful addition to your doll library, but will be an inspiration, enabling you, the doll costumer, to create an infinite number of variations to liven up your doll collection.

We hope that you will not only delight in browsing through the material offered, enjoying the illustrations which carry you back to another century, but that you will be inspired to recreate some of these lovely fashions on your own dolls, thus saving them for posterity.

So do add this book to your library of doll costuming or fashion design, as a convenient reference to the styles of 1890 to 1905. Use the patterns included to costume some of those dolls sitting unclothed in your collection, and enjoy the limitless variations and styles which will liven your doll family, allowing your dolls to put their "best foot forward" with your creations.

*References are primarily to *The Delineator*, a fashion magazine published from 1872 to 1937.

1890 Misses' Costume

Steel gray serge was chosen for the toilette in this instance, and the trimming consists of cream-colored braid, fancy buttons and ribbon. The foundation skirt is in the regulation four-gored style; over it is arranged a drapery that is laid in kilt-plaits at the center, in double box-plaits at the sides and in kilt-plaits back of the box-plaits. Back of the box-plaits, and also in front of them, the drapery is trimmed near the lower edge with three rows of braid, and groups of buttons are ornamentally placed the entire length of the box-plaits. The back-breadth is covered with a straight drapery arranged in two double box-plaits.

The basque has contrasting fronts, which are arranged upon fitted fronts of lining. The right front is in surplice style, having fullness gathered at the shoulder edge and drawn in closely at the lower corner; back of the fullness it is fitted smoothly by a bust dart. A deep, square yoke, which covers the upper part of the left front-lining, is extended to pass under the surplice front; lapping upon it is a full front that

is shirred twice near the upper edge to form a frill, the fullness being collected in plaits at the lower edge. The yoke is decorated with diagonal strips of braid; at the neck is a high standing collar, above which appears a tiny ruching. The stylish sleeves fit smoothly below the elbow, and the fullness above is arranged in gathers in the upper edge and tacked to the coat-shaped linings to produce the soft, upright folds pictured; three rows of braid encircle each wrist. A plaited ribbon is inserted in the right underarm seam, carried about the pointed lower edge of the surplice front and arranged in loops and ends at the front corner. At the back the basque is closely fitted and is deeply pointed at the center.

The mode is adaptable to all sorts of dress fabrics such as cashmere, foulé, tamise, Henrietta cloth, serge, camel's-hair, all-wool Surah, etc.; and the trimming may consist of braid, ribbon, passementerie, velvet ribbon, etc.

This costume was designed for girls from ten to sixteen years of age.

The stylish sailor hat is trimmed with fancy ribbon, which is carried about the crown and bowed at the back.

1890 Ladies' Coat Basque

No. 3127 — Gray camel's hair and moiré are united in this instance; buttons provide the trimming. The backs are closely fitted and formed in slender coat-tails; the stylish jacket-fronts open over a full vest, the fullness of which at the lower edge is confined by a softly folded girdle. A sailor collar that falls squarely at the back is continued along the front edges of the jacket fronts to the bust, with the effect of pointed revers, below which three buttons are ornamentally placed on each front. The standing collar is of regulation height and the sleeves are in shapely coat-sleeve style.

1890 Ladies' Walking Skirt

No. 3142 — Gray camel's hair was employed for making this skirt. The front-drapery, which covers the gores of the regulation four-gored skirt, is laid in a deep, backward-turning plait at each side some distance back of the center, and back of this is arranged a deep, forward-turning plait, all the plaits flaring slightly toward the bottom. The arrangement of the drapery gives the effect of flat panels, which is emphasized by the application of a band of moiré silk to the upper folds of the plaits. On the top of the drapery are arranged fluffy paniers that present a rounding lower outline; a waterfall-drapery is at the back.

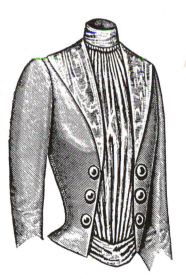

1890 Girls' Dresses

No. 3110 — White wash silk and dark velvet are united in the dress in the present instance and velvet ribbon supplies the decoration. The full round skirt is hemmed at the lower edge and decorated above with several clusters of fine tucks. The upper edge is gathered and joined to the stylish little waist which has a full front and bucks that are gathered at the neck and shoulder edges and also at the lower edges. The full portions are arranged over a smooth front and backs of lining that are joined by underarm and shoulder seams and closed in the back. About the waist is placed a velvet girdle which shapes a decided point in its upper edge at the center of the front and back and adds greatly to the charming effect of the dress. The pattern provides for a standing collar at the neck, which in this case is omitted in favor of a full frill of the material; the coat sleeves which are tucked at the wrists to correspond with the skirt, have shoulder puffs that are each gathered at the upper and lower edges.

The large hat flares stylishly from the face and is trimmed at the back with a spray of flowers and ribbon loops pointing toward the front.

This dress is attractive on two to eight-year-old girls.

No. 3146 — In this instance the dress is pictured made of white fancy tucking and fancy hemstitched flouncing. The full round skirt is made of flouncing and the upper edge is drawn by gathers and sewed to the full waist, which is gathered once at the upper edge and twice at the lower edge both front and back and sewed to the square yoke of the tucking, the closing being made invisibly at the back. Broad sash ties finished at the ends with wide hems are plaited at the under arm seams and arranged in a large bow at the back. At the neck is a standing collar. The full sleeves are gathered at the upper and lower edges and each finished with a cuff.

The picturesque little dress is so simple in construction that its popularity is assured. The mode will develop daintily in all varieties of wash fabrics such as cambric, lawn, mull, all-over embroidery, seersucker, fancy tucking etc.; cashmere, Henrietta cloth, challis and nun's-vailing in all the delicate shades will also make up prettily.

The little bonnet is made of lawn and bordered at its front edge with embroidery.

Pattern No. 3146 can be worn by one to six-year-old girls.

No. 3146

No. 3110

LITTLE GIRLS' DRESS

1891 Ladies' Costume

No. 4092 — The costume is here shown made of *crépe de Chine*, and velvet ribbon and ruffles of the material comprise the decoration. The foundation skirt is fashioned in the approved four-gored style and is concealed beneath a graceful drapery, which is disposed in slight cross folds and wrinkles at the front by three tiny forward-turning, overlapping plaits at each side of the center. The sides of the drapery are rendered smooth over the hips by three shallow, backward-turning plaits at each side, the fullness at the back is collected in fan-plaits which flare in regulation fashion to the edge, and a placket is finished beneath the plaits at the left side. The edge of the drapery is hemmed and is stylishly trimmed with two ruffles of the material finished with French bindings, the upper ruffle being set on to form a self-heading. On one side of the drapery two long strips of velvet ribbon are tacked at the belt and tied in a pretty bow above the ruffles; on the other side one strip is tacked and is also bowed at the bottom.

The basque is cut in low, square outline at the top and is made over a smooth lining that is closely adjusted by double bust darts, under-arm and side-back gores and a curving center seam. It has full center-fronts and a full center-back, which are turned under at the top and shirred to form a pretty standing frill; the fullness below is drawn well to the center by rows of shirring below the waistline. The side edges of the center-fronts and center-back are overlapped by the edges of full side-fronts and side-backs which are seamless on the shoulders. The outer edges of the side portions are turned under the shirred to form frills over the shoulders, and gathers at the arms'-eyes produce a fashionable high puff effect. The fullness at the lower edge of each side-fronts is collected in two forward-turning plaits which overlap the hem and flare prettily toward the top; tuckings made at intervals to the lining secure the artistic arrangement of the plaits. Underarm gores complete the superb adjustment and the closing is made invisibly at the center of the front. The short puff sleeves are turned under at the bottom and shirred to form pretty, drooping frills about the arms; they are arranged upon smooth linings and are gathered at the top to curve stylishly over the shoulders. Frills of velvet ribbon are arranged about the arms'-eyes to complete the picturesque effect. A band of velvet ribbon encircles each sleeve near the lower edge and is arranged in a butterfly bow on the upper side. The pointed lower edge of the basque is ornamented with a narrow doubled frill of the material; bow of velvet ribbon decorates the left side of the front over the ribbon on the skirt.

The mode will develop exquisitely for ball or reception wear in plain and embroidered *mousseline de soie*, *chiffon*, crépon, tulle, faille, bengaline, India silk and Surah. There are also many dainty woolens which will make up well in this way, among them being albatross, vailing, wool crépon and fine French cashmere. Organdy, mull, Swiss, *mousseline de l'Inde* and fine nainsook will make a simple costume for a *débutante*; and ruffles of the material or of *point d'esprit*, tucking, insertion, ribbon or floral garnitures may be applied for decoration in any preferred manner.

4092
Front View.

4092
Back View.

1891 Ladies' Basque

No. 4080 – This basque forms part of a stylish toilette.

Woolen dress goods and velvet are here united in the basque and passementerie and ribbon bows trim it daintily. The fronts are cut away in low, fanciful outline at the top; the front edges separate to reveal high-necked fronts of lining that close at the center with buttons and buttonholes; the fronts and lining portions are closely adjusted by double bust darts taken up together. The back is shaped in low outline as the top to correspond with the fronts and arranged upon high-necked backs of lining; the back is adjusted by a curving center seam taken up with the seam of the lining; the adjustment is completed by underarm gores. A doubled frill of velvet produces a pretty puff effect along the lower edge of the basque, which shapes a well defined point at the center of the front and of the back and arches well over the hips. The coat sleeves are rendered fanciful by puffs of velvet which are arranged to droop prettily at the elbow and are deepened at the back of the arm. The upper edges of the puffs are concealed by sleeve portions which rise with pronounced curves over the shoulders; the wrists are trimmed with passementerie. At the neck is a stylishly high standing collar of velvet. The exposed portions of the lining fronts and back are faced with velvet, and the front and upper edges of the fronts are ornamented with passementerie, which is extended along the upper edge of the back. A butterfly bow of ribbon decorates each shoulder.

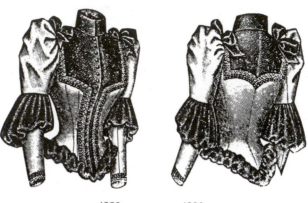

4080
Front View.

4080
Back View.

LADIES' BASQUE. (KNOWN AS THE HOLBEIN WAIST.)

1891 Ladies' Bell Skirt

No. 4078 – Woolen dress goods were here selected for the skirt and machine-stitching and gilt braid supply the decoration. The skirt is fashioned with a front-gore, two side-gores and two back-breadths, all of which are shaped to present the popular bell effect; provision is made for a slight train and also for round length. Three deeply overlapping flounce-draperies are arranged upon the skirt; the lower flounces are disposed without fullness at the top, and the upper flounce is adjusted smoothly over the hips by three darts at each side and is disposed at the back with slight fullness by gathers at each side of the placket, which is made at the seam. The flounces are all straight at the front, and their back edges are bias and are seamed at the center of the back. Tapes are sewed to the side-back seams underneath to draw the fullness to the back as closely as desired. The top of the skirt may be finished with a belt, cording, underfacing or binding, as preferred. The placket is finished at the side-back seam of the skirt. Each flounce is ornamented at the lower edge with a row of gold braid, above which three rows of machine-stitching are applied, with good effect.

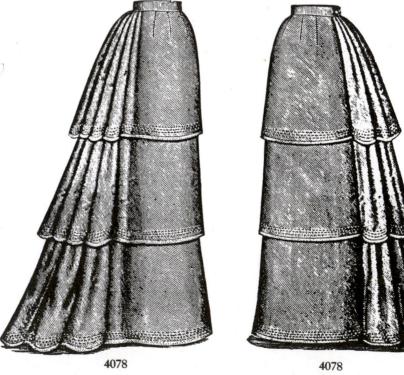

4078
Side-Front View.

4078
Side-Back View.

Lacouriex

Falconer. Imp.Paris

N° 5.027

JOURNAL DES DEMOISELLES, PARIS, February 1895.

JOURNAL DES DEMOISELLES, July, 1895.

JOURNAL DES DEMOISELLES, PARIS, August 1895.

JOURNAL DES DEMOISELLES, PARIS, September 1895.

DER BAZAR, BERLIN, September 1895.

JOURNAL DES DEMOISELLES, PARIS, August 1896.

These two 28in (71cm) Kestners model dropped waist or Russian-bloused dresses. The brown silk satin with ecru lace trim is enhanced with a rose-colored rosette and ribbon belt. The blue moiré silk is a more tailored version with beige lace trim. The dresses feature bishop sleeves ending with a narrow lace ruffle. The sailor hat is trimmed with blue ribbon.

The dresses on this page as well as the following page are variations of the fold-out patterns found in the back of this book. The pattern comes in two sizes for 28in (71cm) and 16½in (42cm) dolls. A lovely ruffled brim hat on a wired frame is included for the 28in doll.

LEFT: This 16½in (42cm) Steiner's dress is shown in English net over pink silk with slightly gathered lace over the skirt. The lace insertion applied to the pleats on the dress front is edged with featherstitching. This trim is repeated on the yoke.

BELOW: This 28in (71cm) Kestner is also attired in a dropped waist or Russian-bloused dress but shows how use of various fabrics and trim can provide quite a different appearance. Here eyelet embroidered fabric is combined with batiste cotton. These same fabrics are used for the hat.

1891
Misses' Dress

No. 3693 — Plain white cotton goods, all-over embroidery and embroidered edging are associated in the dress in the present instance; embroidered flouncing trims it handsomely. The full, round skirt is finished at the bottom with a deep hem, over which falls a ruffle of flouncing finished at the top to form a self-heading. The top of the skirt is gathered and sewed to a band.

The fanciful bodice is closely adjusted by single bust darts, underarm and side-back gores and a curving center seam, and the closing is made at the front with hooks and loops. Disposed over the back and passing into the shoulder seams is an ornamental section of all-over embroidery which extends in a point below the waistline, its edges being sewed to position. A similar section of all-over embroidery is arranged with plastron effect over the front and is included in the right shoulder seam, below which it is permanently sewed to position. Drooping prettily in Bertha fashion over the shoulders are frills of embroidered edging which graduate to points at each end; they extend down the edges of the ornamental sections, below the points of which they are sewed over the basque to the point at the center of the front and back. The front ornamental-section closes at the left shoulder and side edges with hooks and loops, and the left frill is closed invisibly on the left shoulder with buttonholes and tiny lace buttons. The shirt sleeves are gathered at the top and bottom and finished with broad cuffs of edging. A standing collar of all-over embroidery is at the neck, and its ends lap at the center of the front.

Plain and embroidered cashmere, serge and other seasonable wool fabrics, as well as lace gingham, plain and embroidered Swiss, nainsook, percale and all washable textures, will develop nicely by the mode, which is also well adapted to combinations of wool goods with velvet, silk, Surah or Bengaline. Appropriate garnitures of lace, embroidery, ribbon, braid or feather-stitching may be applied in any tasteful way preferred or a simple finish may be adopted. If the dress is made up in wash goods, a very pretty combination may be effected with plain and embroidered chambray.

This dress is designed for young ladies from ten to sixteen years of age.

3693
Front View.

1891
Misses' Dress

No. 3878 — Rose-pink gingham and all-over embroidery are here pictured in the dress. The skirt is full and round and is finished at the bottom with a deep hem; the top is gathered and joined to the fanciful body. The body has a smooth front closely adjusted by single bust darts, over which is arranged a full center-front shaped in low, round outline at the top. The center-front is turned under at the top and shirred to form a frill; the fullness below is collected in two rows of shirring at the lower edge. The backs are shaped by side-back gores and closed invisibly at the center. Full center-backs, which are disposed to correspond with the full center-front, are arranged over the smooth backs, and the side edges of the center-front and center-backs are overlapped at each side by a side-front and side-back which are in one piece. The front and back edges of the side-fronts and side-backs are turned under deeply for hems, back of which they are each arranged in a deep plait turning toward the hem. The side-fronts and side-backs are gathered along the arms'-eyes to form pretty frills over the shoulders, and their side edges pass into the underarm seams. The joining of the skirt and body is concealed by a plaited belt, the ends of which are fastened beneath a large rosette at the center of the back. The coat sleeves, which are mounted on smooth linings, are sufficiently full at the top to curve stylishly over the shoulders, and the wrists are trimmed with deep cuff-facings made of embroidered edging, the scalloped edge of which turns upward. The standing collar is overlaid with narrow edging, and portions of the smooth front and backs exposed in roundyoke shaped are faced with all-over embroidery.

A dress of this kind will develop as tastefully in soft silken and woolen fabrics as in those of washable texture. Dressy effects may be obtained by combining silk, Bengaline or faille with cashmere, serge or challis, and charming dresses for Summer may be developed in plain and embroidered nainsook, batiste or sheer muslin. *Point de Venise* lace, Irish-point embroidery, ribbon, all kinds of braids and passementeries, hemstitching or feather-stitching may be appropriately added for decoration.

This dress is appropriately worn by misses from ten to sixteen years of age.

1891
Girls' Dress

No. 3685 — This dress is shown made of fancy India silk and worn over a silk guimpe.

In the present instance old blue cashmere was selected for the dress. The full, round skirt is finished at the bottom with a deep hem; the top is gathered and joined to the fanciful body, a cording of the material being included in the joining. The front and back of the body are cut away in deep V shape at the top, the adjustment is performed by underarm and side-back gores, and the closing is made at the back with buttonholes and buttons. Over the smooth front is disposed a fanciful front which is drawn by gathers at the shoulder edges; the fullness below is prettily collected at the bust in three cross-rows of rope-shirrings that are made a short distance apart; gathers regulate the fullness at the lower edge. The short puff sleeves

are mounted on smooth linings and are gathered at the top to rise high above the shoulders; the fullness at the lower part is collected in three rows of rope-shirrings to correspond with those in the full front, and the fullness below the shirrings forms a dainty frill about the arm. The plaited ends of sash-ties are included in the underarm seams, and the ties are arranged in a handsome bow at the back.

Surah, Bengaline, serge, challis, etc., will develop attractively by the mode, and so will plain and fancy gingham, percale and other fabrics for summer wear. Dainty feather-stitching done in silk of a prettily contrasting color, or rows of velvet or grosgrain ribbon or of soutache or metallic braid may be added for a foot trimming, or, if preferred, a fine knife-plaiting or a full ruching may be applied. Lace, embroidery or loops of baby ribbon may decorate the body or a plain finish may be adopted.

This dress was designed for five to twelve-year-old girls.

3685
Front View.

1891
Girls' Dress

No. 3697 — The dress is here shown developed in mode and golden brown Henrietta cloth and crochet ball buttons contribute the decoration. The body has a smooth front and back of lining, over the upper part of which square yoke-portions are arranged. The full, round skirt is finished at the bottom with a deep hem and the top is extended to form the body of the dress; it is arranged over the lower part of the smooth body in small tucks that all turn toward the center of the front and extend a little below the lower edge of the smooth portions, from which point the tucks flare prettily into the full folds of the skirt. The closing is made invisibly and an ornamental row of buttons is placed on the overlapping closing edge of the yoke and at the center of the yoke in front. The full puff sleeves are gathered at the top and bottom; the coat-shaped linings

3685
Back View.

over which they are made are exposed to deep cuff depth at the wrists and finished with cuff facings, which are each ornamented at the inside of the arm with a row of crochet buttons. Similar buttons decorate the edge of the collar, which is in standing style. Arranged upon the yoke and following its square outline is a dainty frill of the light material; the frill is extended at each side of the closing and crossed with unique effect, its ends being fastened with hooks and loops under the arms.

Attractive combinations of plaid, figured or striped wool goods with plain fabrics may be effected by the mode, which is also well adapted to the association of silken and woolen textures or to the development of a single material. Braid or feather-stitching may be applied to the skirt for a foot trimming, and any arrangement of gimp, galloon, coarse lace, braiding or fancy stitching may decorate the yoke and cuff facings.

Five to twelve-year-old girls can wear this dress prettily.

3878
Front View.

3878
Back View.

1891
Girls' Dress

No. 4463 — Light serge and velvet are stylishly combined in this dress in Figure No. 501 T. Plain gingham and plaid gingham cut bias are united in the second version. The full skirt is of plain gingham and is trimmed above its deep hem with a broad bias band of plaid gingham; the top of the skirt is gathered and joined to the body, except for a short distance at the front, where it is sewed to a band and attached to the body with hooks and loops, the placket being finished at the left side. The fronts of the body are arranged upon dart-fitted fronts of lining. They are drawn by gathers at the top and the fullness at the lower edge is collected in a short row of gathers at each side of the closing which is made down the center of the front with hooks and loops. The back is seamless at the center and is gathered to correspond with the fronts and arranged over a plain back of lining that is also seamless at the center. Encircling the waist is a girdle of plaid gingham, the upper edge of which is pointed at the center of the front and back. It is quite narrow at the sides and is shaped by a seam at the right side. Its ends are closed at the left side with hooks and loops. The lower ends of the suspenders are tacked underneath the top of the girdle at each side of the center of the front and back. Their upper ends pass into the shoulder seams. The full puff sleeves are gathered at the top and bottom. They are mounted upon coat-shaped linings which are exposed to deep cuff depth at the wrists and finished with cuff facings of the plaid gingham cut bias. At the neck is a pretty sailor collar which falls deep at the back. Its ends flare prettily at the throat.

Plain and spotted percale, embroidered and plain nainsook or chambray, and plain and fancy gingham will develop charmingly by the mode. Applied decoration will not be necessary. All sorts of seasonable woolens are also adapted to the mode and, if a more fanciful completion be desired, braid, gimp, lace, featherstitching or ribbon may be applied in any pretty way suggested by personal fancy. The girdle and suspenders may be all-over decorated with an embroidery edge.

Pattern No. 4463 is appropriately worn by girls from five to twelve years of age.

3697
Front View.

3697
Back View.

4463
Front View.

4463
Back View.

501 T

1891 Girls' Dresses

Figure No. 489P — This consists of a little girl's dress and guimpe, No. 3856.

The dress is here pictured developed in plain nainsook, silk and embroidered flouncing and edging. The skirt is round and full and falls in pretty folds from the body, to which it is joined. The body is low-necked and sleeveless and is arranged upon smooth linings. The front is disposed with pretty fullness at the center, and the backs are arranged to correspond at each side of the closing. A frill of embroidered edging is arranged in bertha fashion over each shoulder; the ends of the frills, which are graduated almost to points, nearly meet at the center of the front and back. A frill of narrow edging droops prettily from the low neck, and the ends of a silk sash that encircles the waist are concealed beneath a rosette of ribbon at the left side.

The guimpe is made of mull. It has a full, seamless yoke arranged over the upper part and effectively disclosed above the top of the dress body; the fullness is nicely drawn to the figure at the waistline by a tape or elastic inserted in a casing. The shirt sleeves are finished with wristbands, from each of which a frill droops over the hand; the standing collar is overlaid with edging.

India or China silk, Surah, mull, Swiss and all other dainty cotton fabrics may be used in developing a dress of this kind. Challis, cashmere, serge and similar seasonable woolens are also adapted in the mode, and feather-stitching, ribbon, embroidery, etc., may be daintily applied for decoration. The guimpe may be made of silk, Surah or any cotton fabric.

This dress was designed for girls from age two to twelve.

Figure No. 490P — Plain and figured India silk are here associated in the dress; dark-blue velvet ribbon provides dainty garniture. The full skirt falls in natural folds from the low-necked, sleeveless body, to which it is joined; the lower edge is finished with a deep hem. Pointed sections of velvet ribbon are arranged in tab fashion about the low, round neck of the body; the closing is made with buttons and buttonholes at the back. The guimpe is adjusted in the ordinary way and closed at the back. A seamless yoke is arranged with pretty fullness over the upper part of the guimpe; a tape inserted in a casing at the waistline draws the garment well to the figure. The shirt sleeves are stylishly full. Each is finished with a wristband, from which a frill of embroidered edging droops prettily over the hand. The standing collar is ornamented with similar edging. A Marguerite pouch or pocket is suspended by dark blue ribbon at the right side.

Effective combinations of shades and textures may be achieved in the dress, and a single color or fabric may be used throughout, with equally tasteful results. Plain, figured or striped China silk, foulard or Surah will be especially dainty; the numerous plain, striped and lace ginghams, percales, chambrays and sheer muslins will also make up attractively in this way. Figured challis, with plain India silk for the guimpe, will develop quaintly by the mode, and feather-stitching done in silk matching the predominating color in the goods will furnish tasteful garniture.

Attractive in this dress from pattern No. 3875 are two to six-year-old girls.

Figure No. 491P — This consists of a little girl's dress and guimpe, No. 3880.

In the present instance the dress is shown made of white mull and embroidered edging. The full, round skirt falls in natural folds from gathers at the top, where it is joined to the low-necked body. The body is closely adjusted in the ordinary manner and closed at the back with buttons and buttonholes. A frill of embroidered edging is arranged in bertha fashion over the shoulders; the frills narrow almost to points at the front and back, and between their tapering ends a puffing of the mull is effectively revealed. A frill of narrow edging and a narrow band conceal the gathered edges of the frills; the top of the puffing is similarly ornamented. A full rosette decorates the lower edge of the body at each side of the center. The short puff sleeves are gathered to narrow bands at the lower edge, each band being decorated with ribbon arranged in a pretty bow at the back of the arm; a frill of edging forms a pretty edge finish.

The guimpe, which is also made of mull, has a full, seamless yoke, which is disclosed in an effective manner above the low-necked body of the dress; and the fullness of the guimpe is drawn nicely to the figure at the waistline by a tape or elastic inserted in a casing. The full shirt-sleeves are gathered to wristbands and trimmed with frills of embroidered edging; similar edging ornaments the standing collar.

Figured India silk or French challis will be especially effective in a dress of this kind, and the guimpe may be of plain silk, nainsook or mull. Embroidered cashmere or nainsook flouncing will also develop attractively by the mode, and lace or embroidered edging, feather-stitching, novelty bands or ribbon may be used as lavishly as desired for garniture.

Girls from two to twelve years of age may wear this toilette.

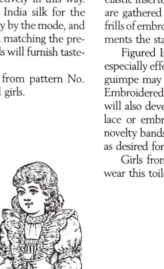

Figure No. 489P   Figure No. 490P   Figure No. 491P

1891
Girls' Dress

No. 3864 — This consists of a little girl's dress and guimpe.

The dress, which is in the quaint Greenaway style, is here portrayed developed in polka-dotted cashmere. It is shaped in low, round outline at the top and is drawn by shirrings to form a pretty standing frill about the neck, below which the fullness falls unconfined to the hemmed lower edge. The dress is shaped by underarm seams and arranged over a short body, which is closed invisibly at the back. The short sleeves are very full and are arranged by gathers and tackings to stand with high puff effect over their smooth linings, and the fullness at the lower edge of each is shirred to form a drooping frill about the arm. A plaited ribbon tacked at the center of the front and at the underarm seams, confines the fullness at the top in a unique manner; a large silk rosette at the back conceals the ends of the ribbon, and a similar rosette decorates the center of the front and covers the plaited ends of ribbons, which fall gracefully almost to the edge of the dress.

The guimpe is made of mull. A full, seamless yoke is arranged over the upper part; the fullness in the plain front and back is nicely conformed to the figure at the waistline by a tape or drawstring. The shirt sleeves are each finished with a wristband, from which a dainty frill of edging droops prettily over the hand; a frill of similar edging is at the neck.

India or China silk, Surah, challis and cashmere will develop with especially dainty effect in the dress, which may be made up for various purposes in all seasonable silks, woolens and cottons. For garniture a simple arrangement of ribbon, lace, embroidery or feather-stitching will be appropriate, or, if preferred, the finish may be perfectly plain. The guimpe may be made of lace, net, Swiss, tucking, lawn or nainsook. The dress may be worn without the guimpe, if a low-necked, short-sleeve dress be desired.

This dress is effectively worn by girls two to eight years old.

The hat is a large shape in fine straw prettily trimmed with loops of ribbon.

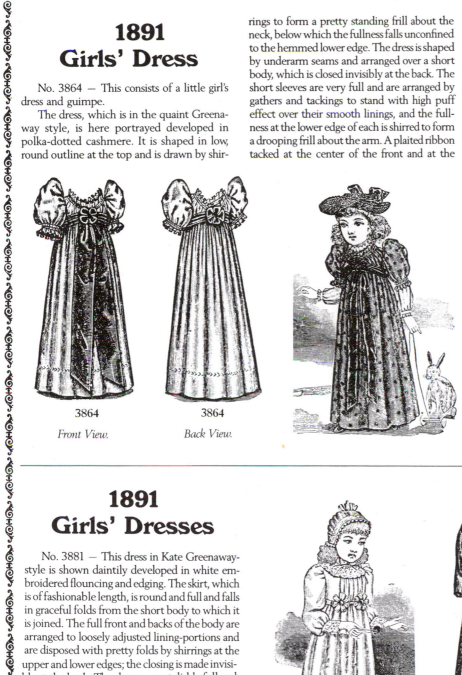

3864
Front View.

3864
Back View.

1891
Girls' Dresses

No. 3881 — This dress in Kate Greenaway-style is shown daintily developed in white embroidered flouncing and edging. The skirt, which is of fashionable length, is round and full and falls in graceful folds from the short body to which it is joined. The full front and backs of the body are arranged to loosely adjusted lining-portions and are disposed with pretty folds by shirrings at the upper and lower edges; the closing is made invisibly at the back. The sleeves are stylishly full and the linings over which they are made are finished in deep cuff cotton with embroidered edging. A frill of similar edging finishes the neck. A rosette of ribbon ornaments the front at each side of the center; from beneath each rosette a section of ribbon is carried to the center of the back where the ribbons are tied in a pretty bow, the long loops and ends of which fall gracefully over the skirt.

Embroidered and plain nainsook, batiste or chambray will develop attractively by the mode; equally dainty dresses may be made of plaid, checked, striped or lace gingham. Cashmere, merino, French serge and challis will also make up prettily in this way. A pretty garniture of feather-stitching, velvet or grosgrain ribbon, *point de Géne* lace or Irish-point embroidery may be added.

Girls from two to six years of age look darling in this frock.

The becoming bonnet is made of silk trimmed with ribbon and fancy braid.

3881
Front View.

3881
Back View.

1892 Ladies' Costume

Figures Nos. 478 T and 479 T. — These two figures illustrate the same pattern — Ladies' costume No. 4510.

At figure No. 478 T the costume is pictured made up in turquoise-blue glacé Surah and Kursheedt's Standard black striped drapery net. The graceful bell skirt is made with a short train, which, if objectionable, may be cut off, the pattern also providing for a skirt of round length. The skirt has a circular bell foundation-skirt and is gathered slightly across the top at the front and sides. The back is disposed in backward-turning plaits at each side of the seam uniting the bias back edges. The skirt is decorated near the bottom with two rows of turquoise-blue ribbon drawn through slashes made at intervals and the lower edge is finished with a hem-facing.

The fanciful basque has full fronts, the right one of which is widened to cross in surplice fashion. The fullness in these fronts below the bust is collected in closely lapped plaits; the upper edges flare widely below a yoke of Surah, which is disposed in soft folds by gathers at the top and bottom and is arranged upon dartfitted fronts of lining that close invisibly at the center. The full back is cut away in V shape at the top to accommodate a full, pointed yoke arranged upon a closely adjusted back of lining; the fullness below the waistline is plaited to a point at the lower edge; underarm gores produce a becoming smooth adjustment at the sides. Bertha frills of net fall with quaint effect from the upper edges of the full fronts and back, and a standing collar is at the neck. The leg-o'-mutton sleeves rise fashionably above the shoulders and are arranged upon smooth coat-shaped linings, and each wrist is decorated with three rows of narrow ribbon and three butterfly bows of similar ribbon. The pointed lower edge of the basque is followed with ribbon matching that upon the skirt; a full rosette-bow, from which long loops and ends fall prettily over the skirt, is placed at the left side.

Figure No. 479 T represents a back view of the costume developed in white India silk. The yoke is omitted, and the lining is cut away in low-pointed outline. The upper and lower edges of the basque and the bottom of the skirt are decorated with three rows of yellow velvet ribbon, and bows of similar ribbon having long loops and ends droop prettily from the upper and lower edges of the basque at the center. The sleeves are cut off just below the elbows and rows and bows of yellow ribbon trim their lower edges.

A sumptuous dinner gown may be developed by the mode in *crêpe de Chine*, crépon, figured or plain India silk, foulard or any preferred variety of softly clinging wool goods. Ribbon, frills of lace or *chiffon*, passementerie, embroidery, etc., will contribute effective garniture.

Figure No. 478 T.

Figure No. 479 T.

1892 Ladies' Costume

No. 4408 — Figured and plain India silk are here beautifully combined in the costume, which is composed of a fancy bodice and a slightly draped bell skirt. A four-gored foundation-skirt underlies the skirt, which is made with bias back edges that are joined in a seam at the center of the back in regular bell fashion. At the left side the skirt opens from the belt down, the edges flaring gradually toward the foot, to attractively reveal a deep facing of plain silk applied to the left side of the foundation skirt. The flaring edges are widely hemmed and are connected by ribbons extending diagonally from under the hem on the front portion and tied in bows that are tacked upon the opposite hem. A jabot of lace edging extends down the front hem, near which a cluster of three plaits turn toward the center at the belt and flare into pretty, draping folds below. Just back of the other hem two backward-turning plaits are laid at the belt; a group of three overlapping, forward-turning plaits are laid in front of gathers across the back, the plaits flaring diagonally forward in graceful, draping folds, while the

gathers fall naturally to the edge of the slight train. Small plaits on the hips fit the top instead of darts. If the trained skirt be undesirable, the skirt and foundation may be shortened to round length.

The bodice is made up on a lining fitted by double bust darts, underarm and side-back gores and a curving center seam. On the lining fronts are placed a full vest and surplice fronts. The vest extends only to the waistline and is gathered at the neck and laid in forward-turning plaits at the lower edge; it is closed at the center like the lining fronts and is sewed to position at its edges. The surplice fronts lap in the regular way below the waistline and separate above to the shoulders over the vest. At the lower edge each surplice front is laid in three forward-turning plaits that are folded even with the front edge and flare gradually toward the bust, where they fall out of their formal folds into soft fullness, which is collected in gathers at the shoulder edges. The right front crosses the left below the bust and takes the shape of the basque at the lower edge, which describes a becoming point at the center. A full center-back arranged upon the back lining is gathered at the neck and plaited to a point below the waistline; it is over-lapped by full

backs, which spread to the shoulders, where they are gathered with pretty effect. Below the waistline the full backs are drawn smoothly over the lining and the fullness is collected in two backward-turning plaits over the hemmed back edges, which are trimmed with jabots of lace edging that is carried across the shoulders and in jabots down the front edges of the surplice fronts. A pretty tied bow of ribbon is placed on the center of the back at the waistline; loops and ends of ribbon fall with graceful effect from beneath the point of the back. The stylish collar stands high and is softly rolled at the top, its corners being prettily rounded. The sleeves are in the becoming leg-o'-mutton style, flaring full and broadly at the top and taking the shape of the arm below the elbow. They are made over coat-shaped linings and are each daintily trimmed at the wrist with a lace frill and ribbon that is carried diagonally across the under side and tied in a bow at the seam.

For the light, soft textures so delightful for house wear the costume will be particularly charming. It may be simply or elaborately trimmed with any of the seasonable garnitures in vogue or it may be perfectly plain in finish.

4408

4408
Right Side-Front View.

4408
Left Side-Back View.

1892
Misses' Dress

No. 4498 — The dress is here shown prettily developed in challis. The full skirt is finished at the bottom with a deep hem, above which five rows of narrow velvet ribbon are ornamentally applied. It is mounted on a four-gored foundation-skirt, which, however, may be omitted; the top is gathered and joined to the round body. The body has a smooth lining adjusted by single bust darts and underarm and side-back gores and closed at the back with buttonholes and buttons. The full front and backs are drawn at the top by four rows of shirring arranged some distance apart to outline a round yoke, and the fullness below is drawn to the center of the front and back and collected in four short rows of shirring made close together. Underarm gores produce a becoming, smooth adjustment at the sides. Bertha frills that are very broad on the shoulders and are narrowed almost to point at the ends are arranged upon the body; their free edges are decorated with three rows of velvet ribbon. The full puff sleeves are gathered at the top and bottom and are arranged upon smooth, coat-shaped linings which are exposed to cuff depth at the wrists and finished with cuff facings of challis trimmed at the edge with five encircling rows of velvet ribbon; four rows of similar ribbon decorate the standing collar.

Figured and polka-dotted challis, cashmere, serge and novelty wool suitings will make up attractively in this way, and so will fancy and plain gingham, percale, nainsook and other washable goods. The Bertha frills may be of some contrasting material or of embroidered edging, and feather-stitching, braid, ribbon or lace may contribute dainty garniture.

This is an attractive costume for misses from eight to sixteen years of age.

4498

Front View.

4498

Back View.

1892
Misses' Costume

No. 4404 — Hair-striped gingham and all-over embroidery are here prettily united in the dress, and embroidered edging is the decoration selected. The skirt is full and round and is finished at the bottom with a deep hem; the top is gathered and joined to the round body. The body has a full front, which is cut in slightly low, round outline at the top and is gathered at the upper and lower edges for a short distance at each side of the center. The front is arranged upon a high-necked front of lining adjusted by single bust darts. The full backs are arranged to correspond with the full front and are mounted in a similar manner on backs of lining shaped by side-back gores and closed invisibly at the center; underarm gores complete the adjustment. That portion of the lining exposed to shallow, round yoke depth at the front and back is covered with a yoke facing of all-over embroidery, from beneath which the linings may be cut away. From the top of the full front and backs a frill of wide embroidered edging droops, with pretty effect. The full puff sleeves are gathered at the top and bottom and droop in characteristic fashion over deep cuff-facings of all-over embroidery applied to the coat-shaped linings over which they are made. A frill of narrow edging decorates each wrist edge, and the standing collar is cut from embroidered edging. The waist is encircled by a girdle, the upper edge of which is pointed at the center of the front. At the back and sides the girdle is of belt depth, the closing being made at the left side with hooks and loops; the upper and lower edges are trimmed with narrow embroidered edging.

The mode is particularly well adapted to washable goods of all varieties, checked, striped and figured gingham, nainsook, percale and lawn being especially pretty when made up in this way. Fancy tucking and insertion, all-over embroidery, lace, etc., may form the yoke and cuff facings, and feather-stitching, embroidery, fancy braid, ribbon, lace, etc., may contribute additional garniture.

Misses from ten to sixteen can effectively wear this dress.

1892 Girls' Dress

No. 4778 — In the present instance a dainty combination of cashmere and silk was selected for the dress. The round skirt is deeply hemmed at the bottom and falls in full, soft folds from gathers at the top, where it is joined to the body. The body has a full front which is arranged upon a smooth front of lining and appears with blouse effect between the flaring edges of jacket fronts that are prettily rounded and trimmed with two rows of jet gimp. Underarm and side-back gores complete the simple adjustment of the body and the closing is made at the center of the back with buttonholes and buttons. The puff sleeves extend below the elbows and droop with picturesque fullness over deep cuff-facings which are applied to the smooth, coat-shaped linings and decorated with four evenly spaced encircling rows of jet gimp. The upper and lower edges of the standing collar are trimmed to correspond. The waist is encircled by a ribbon sash, the ends of which fall low upon the skirt.

Pretty combination of colors or materials may be effected in the development of the dress, and partly worn dresses may be easily renovated by the mode. Crépon, serge, vienna or cashmere may be combined with silk, faille or China silk, and braid, Russian bands, feather-stitching, ribbon or gimp may be applied for garniture in any pretty way preferred.

Pattern No. 4778 is for girls from five to twelve years old.

4404
Front View.

4404
Back View.

4778
Front View.

4778
Back View.

1892 Girls' Dress

No. 4427 — Olive-brown cashmere and old-pink silk are here associated in the dress, with pretty effect. The full round skirt falls in natural folds from gathers at the top; the lower edge is finished with a deep hem and decorated with a silk ruffle finished to form a self-heading. The skirt is joined to the body, a cording of the material being included in the joining. The body is arranged upon a lining fitted by shoulder and underarm seams. It has a full center-front and center-backs that are shaped in low, round outline at the top and joined in short seams on the shoulders. The fullness of the center-backs and center-front is drawn by a shirring near the upper edge to form a standing frill at the top, and in slight gathers at the arms'-eyes. The fullness at the lower edge is collected in four forward-turning plaits at each side of the center of the front and at each side of the closing, which is made invisibly at the back. Smooth side-fronts and side-backs pass into the underarm seams and lap upon the center-front and center-backs; the exposed part of the lining is covered by full yoke-portions of silk that are gathered at their upper and lower edges. The shoulder edges of the yoke portions center the shoulder seams, and the lower edges are sewed beneath the frill of the center-front and center-back; a cording and a standing frill of silk are at the neck. The full shirt-sleeves are gathered at the top and bottom and are finished with wristbands.

The mode may be attractively developed in cashmere, flannel, foulé, serge and similar soft woolens, combined with silk, Surah, China silk or faille. The dress will make up prettily for party wear in all evening shades, and ruffles of lace, embroidered *chiffon* of the material may be chosen for the skirt decoration.

This is an attractive dress for girls from five to twelve years of age.

1893
Ladies' Dresses

No. 6314 — The costume is especially good style for visiting, driving, theatre and other dressy wear, and is here presented in an effective combination of white and red India silk. The skirt is fashioned in the popular circular Empire style and displays the flaring effect characteristic of the mode, with a becomingly smooth and close adjustment at the top of the front and sides. The fullness at the back is drawn closely to the center in long, rolling flutes or folds by gathers at the top, the flutes spreading all the way down and concealing the seam joining their straight back edges. The skirt is decorated at the bottom, just below the knee and halfway between with bands of red silk ornamented with a fanciful arrangement of white silk soutache braid.

The round waist suggests the picturesque Empire modes and will be found especially becoming to slender figures. Its full fronts are arranged upon dart-fitted fronts of lining, and are disposed in a succession of pretty folds between boléros which round prettily at their lower edges and are decorated with white silk soutache in a design like that on the skirt. The full back is arranged to correspond with the full fronts over a fitted back of lining; underarm gores produce desirable smoothness at the sides and the closing is made invisibly at the center of the front. The waist is encircled by a broad Empire girdle that is disposed in soft folds and wrinkles all round and closed invisibly at the left side; the standing collar is overlaid with a crush collar closed at the left shoulder seam. Empire puffs appear upon the coat sleeves and give breadth to the shoulders; each wrist is trimmed with an encircling band of red silk ornamented with soutache braid.

An exquisite costume for afternoons at home, formal luncheons and other semi-ceremonious occasions may be developed in Bengaline, Ondine, taffeta, bourette grenadine, India silk or any of the fashionable silk-and-wool novelty goods; the decoration of the skirt and boléros may be supplied by rich passementerie, rare lace or handsome embroideries. For more serviceable wear ribbon, Hercules braid, gimp, bourdon insertion or edging, milliners' folds, etc., will provide stylish and becoming garniture.

4427
Front View.

4427
Back View.

No. 6315

No. 6314

The hat is a smart shape in fancy straw simply adorned with aigrettes and silk.

No. 6315 — The costume introduces a blouse effect, a fanciful girdle and bretelles, and is here portrayed developed in réséda camel's-hair and shell pink India silk. The four-gored skirt presents the fashionable flare at the bottom and a rather close adjustment at the top of the front and sides; the fullness is massed at the center of the back in long, rolling folds or flutes that spread gracefully to the lower edge, which is decorated with two frills of the material headed by a band of *point de Géne* lace, which in turn is surmounted with a self-headed frill of the material.

The fanciful round basque is arranged upon a closely adjusted body-lining that is closed invisibly at the center of the front. Its full center-fronts of India silk are plaited to a point at the lower edge, the fullness flaring upward into soft folds between smooth side-fronts, which reach a trifle below the bust and are overlapped at the bottom by a fanciful girdle overlaid with *point de Gène* lace. The full center-back appears with the effect of a full, pointed yoke between the flaring edges of the smooth backs, and the back of the girdle meets the center-back in a deep point. Bretelles covered with *point de Gène* edging droop in full, soft folds over the shoulders, and their smooth ends, which taper to points, extend to the points of the girdle at the front and back. To carry out the blouse effect, the full puff-sleeves are made of India silk. They are arranged upon smooth, coat-shaped linings, which are covered below the puffs with round cuff-facings of camel's-hair overlaid with *point de Gène* lace. At the neck is a rolling collar, between the flaring ends of which a figured silk scarf is prettily bowed.

The costume is one of the most fanciful of the new modes, but possesses an elegance which will recommend it to women of quiet tastes. Étamine, velours, hopsacking, *épingeline*, serge or novelty wool goods may be associated with rainbow silk, changeable Surah, India silk, etc., in a costume of this kind; or a single material of either silken or woolen texture may be used throughout. Bourdon lace, passementerie, gimp or galloon may be added for decoration, or a less elaborate completion may be chosen.

The fanciful straw hat is quaintly bent and is garnitured at the front with marguerites and a loop and standing ends of ribbon.

6315
Front View.

6315
Back View.

6314
Front View.

6314
Side-Back View.

1893
Ladies' Dress

No. 6313 — A charming costume for morning or traveling wear is here represented, the materials being plain and fancy novelty wool goods. The skirt flares in the accepted style, and consists of seven gores, which are shaped to fit the figure at the top of the front and sides with the becoming closeness of the bell styles, and are widened below to produce fashionable fullness at the bottom. The fullness at the back is collected in coarse gathers at the top, from which it falls in a series of rolling folds or flutes that spread in graceful fashion to the bottom; the skirt is trimmed some distance above the lower edge with a broad band of plain goods, upon which numerous evenly spaced rows of soutache braid are arranged. A placket is finished at the left side-front seam, and the top of the skirt is joined to the body, the joining being concealed by a broad belt which is decorated with rows of braid and closed invisibly at the left side. The body has loose fronts and a seamless back arranged upon a body lining that is adjusted by the customary darts and seams. The right front of lining is extended above the bust to the left shoulder seam and is faced with the contrasting material to simulate a chemisette; the fronts lap in surplice fashion below the bust. The fullness at the lower edges is drawn to the center and collected in gathers made at belt depth apart, and the fullness at the lower edge of the seamless back is disposed in a similar manner. The waist has a lapel-collar which rolls deeply at the back, is notched on the shoulders and extends in long, tapering ends to the lower edges of the fronts; above the lapel-collar is a close-fitting standing collar that closes at the left shoulder seam. The standing collar is decorated with upright rows of soutache braid arranged in line with rows of braid which ornament the simulated chemisette and two rows of braid follow the edges of the lapel-collar. The coat sleeves are of the fashionable mutton-leg shape. They are mounted upon smooth linings, and each is trimmed at the wrist with a broad encircling band of the contrasting goods overlaid with rows of braid.

6313
Front View.

6313
Back View.

1893 Girls' Dress and Misses' Eton Costume

No. 6354 — Plain and striped Surah and edging are united in this dress with insertion for trimming.

Mode cashmere and cherry silk are here effectively combined in the dress, which introduces so pleasingly a full yoke, Bertha-bretelles and bishop sleeves. The full skirt is of regulation depth and is finished at the bottom with a deep hem; it is gathered at the top and falls in soft, flowing folds from the fanciful waist, which has a high-necked body-lining that is smoothly adjusted by underarm gores, and closed invisibly at the center of the back. Arranged upon the upper part of the lining is a full, seamless yoke that is gathered at the lower edge and turned under at the top and shirred twice to form a pretty standing frill at the neck. The front and back of the waist are shaped in low, round outline at the top to reveal the yoke, and are separated by underarm gores. The closing is made at the center of the back being invisible along the yoke and made with buttonholes and buttons below. Gathered Bertha-bretelles of the cashmere fall gracefully from the upper edge of the waist and form a becoming completion; if, however, they be deemed undesirable, they may be omitted as shown in the small illustration. The bishop sleeves, always so quaint and picturesque, are mounted on coat-shaped linings, which are revealed at the wrists with round-cuff effect; they are gathered at the top and bottom and fall in pretty folds from the shoulders, and the exposed portions of the linings are faced with the material.

This dress is appropriate for girls from three to twelve years of age.

6354
View Without Bertha-Bretelle.

6354
Front View.

6354
Back View.

6355
View without Jacket.

6355
Front View.

6355
Back View.

No. 6354   No. 6355

1893 Misses' Costume

No. 6355 — *Vieux-rose* figured India silk is combined with gray cheviot in this costume.

The Eton modes are still popular for outing and yachting toilettes and for general wear in the city or country. A charming example of this favorite mode is here pictured made up in blue serge and figured silk. The skirt is of the new full, flaring variety and consists of a front-gore, a gore at each side and a wide back-gore. The very slight fullness at the top of the front and sides is collected in gathers; the back is closely gathered to fall in full flutes or folds that spread, in a decided flare, to the lower edge. **The skirt is fashionably wide and is decorated at the lower edge and again nearly half way to the top with a row of rather wide white Hercules braid, each row being headed by two rows of narrow braid; two rows of narrow braid trim the upper and lower edges of the belt.**

The blouse is adjusted by shoulder and underarm seams and closed at the center of the front with buttonholes and buttons. The fronts display slight fullness at each side of the closing resulting from gathers at the top; the top of the back is similarly gathered at the center. The fullness at the waistline of the back is drawn closely to the center by a shirr-tape which is inserted in a casing and tied over the fronts. The sleeves are in leg-o'-mutton style with inside seams only; they are made with fashionable fullness at the top and are smooth and comfortably close-fitting below the elbows. At the neck is a moderately high standing collar covered with folds of the material.

The removable Eton jacket is fashionably short and its loose fronts and seamless back are joined in shoulder and underarm seams. The fronts are reversed in very broad lapels that meet a deep, Empire rolling collar in notches. The coat sleeves rise full and high on the shoulders and are sufficiently wide below the elbow to slip on easily over the blouse sleeves. The collar, lapels and wrists are trimmed with a row of wide braid and two rows of narrow braid, and the lower and front edges of the jacket are decorated with two rows of narrow braid.

The costume presents the natty effect characteristic of the Eton modes and may be developed in French yachting serge, storm serge, flannel, outing cloth, hopsacking, cheviot, camel's-hair, linen, duck, piqué, etc., with plain or fancy silk, wash silk, percale, French batiste or linen lawn for the blouse. Garniture may be supplied by Hercules or soutache braid, or a plain tailor finish of machine-stitching may be chosen. The closing of the blouse will often be performed with studs instead of with buttons and buttonholes.

Young ladies from ten to sixteen years of age will look attractive in this design.

1893
Misses' Dresses

No. 6343 — The costume is very stylish in effect, but is remarkably simple in construction. In the present instance it is shown made of cashmere and silk in two widely contrasting shades of réséda. The skirt is in the four-gored Empire style and presents slight fullness at the top of the front and sides, while the fullness at the back is arranged in coarsely drawn gathers that produce pretty curved folds to the lower edge. Three tiny frills of silk form a stylish foot-trimming, the upper one being finished to form a self-heading.

The waist is worn beneath the skirt and has full fronts and a full back, which are arranged over a body lining fitted by single bust darts and underarm and side-back gores and a curving center seam; the closing is made invisibly at the center of the front. The back fits smoothly across the shoulders and is drawn in to the figure at the waistline by a short row of shirring, and the fullness of the fronts is prettily disposed by gathers at the neck and waistline. Arranged upon the waist are short jacket-fronts of the material, which flare broadly toward the shoulders and reveal the fronts with full vest effect. Gathered bretelles, that are very broad over the shoulders and taper to points at their front ends, droop softly over the sleeves and extend down the front edges of the jacket fronts; their back ends are tacked to the back near the arms'-eyes. Balloon puffs reaching midway to the elbow are arranged over the coat-shaped sleeves; the puffs are gathered at the top and bottom and fall in numberless broken folds; the sleeves, which closely follow the outline of the arm, are each trimmed at the wrist with a self-headed frill of silk. Similar frills outline the bretelles. The standing collar is concealed by a wrinkled section of silk; the waist is encircled by a crush belt which is closed at the back under a fanciful bow consisting of a knot and pointed ends.

This is an attractive costume for misses from ten to sixteen years old.

The straw hat flares becomingly over the face and is tastefully trimmed with ribbons and plumes.

No. 6326 — A pretty color combination was effected in the present development of the dress, the materials selected being cream vailing and red silk, with lace insertion for decoration. Insertion is a very popular trimming this season, being used on woolens as well as cottons. The skirt extends to the approved depth for misses' garments and is in the popular four-gored Empire style. It is handsomely trimmed at hem depth from the lower edge with a band of red silk overlaid with lace insertion. The top is gathered and joined to the fanciful body, only enough fullness being allowed at the front and sides to secure an easy adjustment over the hips. The full front and full backs of the body are shaped in low V outline at the top and are separated by underarm gores. They are arranged over a high-necked body-lining fitted by single bust darts and underarm and side-back gores; the closing is made invisibly at the center of the back. The low-necked portions are gathered at the top and bottom at the center of the front and at each side of the closing, and the lining above them is faced, to simulate a deep pointed yoke, with silk covered with vertical rows of lace insertion. The close-fitting standing collar of silk is similarly ornamented. Gathered bretelles, that are fashionably broad on the shoulders and taper to points at the ends, fall from the neck edge of the low-necked portions; their free edges are tastefully trimmed with silk and insertion, and their ends meet in points at the bust and at the center of the back. Very full Empire puffs that extend midway to the elbows are arranged over the smooth, coat-shaped sleeves, each of which is trimmed at the wrist with a band of insertion applied upon red silk. The waist is encircled by a crush girdle, the ends of which are turned under and shirred to form frills.

Exquisite dresses may be fashioned by the mode in embroidered or Bulgarian flouncing, mull, dotted Swiss, organdy, challis or fine figured crépon, and lace, embroidery or ribbon may be selected for garniture. A pretty skirt-decoration consists of three lace frills headed with quillings of ribbon or with a band of three-line beading through which *bébé* ribbon is interlaced, the ribbon being arranged at intervals in coquettish little rosette-bows or loose knots.

Ten to sixteen-year-old misses wear this dress effectively.

The large hat is of fine light straw trimmed with ribbons and heather.

No. 6343

No. 6326

1893 Girls' Dresses

No. 6394 — The dress introduces the ever-popular smocking with quaint effect, and is here portrayed made up in a dainty combination of écru Henrietta cloth and Havane changeable silk. The full, round skirt is extended to form the full front and full backs of the fanciful body, which flare widely to reveal full yoke-portions of silk arranged upon a closely adjusted body of lining. The front and backs are gathered up closely on the shoulders to produce soft folds below; the fullness at the waistline is smocked to broad belt depth, the skirt falling below in full, soft folds all round to the lower edge, where it is deeply hemmed. The coat sleeves have full puffs which extend to the elbow and are smocked to cap depth at the top, the fullness below drooping in the quaint style of the 1830 modes. A silk standing collar is at the neck and the dress is closed invisibly at the center of the back.

The dress, which is extremely graceful, offers opportunity for successful combinations of shades and textures. It will make up exquisitely in India or China silk in two harmonizing shades, or in cashmere and rainbow silk, vicuna and Surah, or plain or figured challis and plaid silk. The mode is so decorative in effect that applied garniture is not really necessary, but it is a pretty fancy to make the smocking with silk of a daintily contrasting color. An attractive gown of this kind may be fashioned from red wool batiste and white silk powdered with red figures; the smocking may be done with white silk.

Three to twelve-year-old girls wear this dress attractively.

No. 6406 — The dress is one of the quaintest styles lately devised for girls' wear, suggesting, as it does in a marked manner, the picturesque effect of the short-waisted Empire modes. It is here shown developed in an artistic combination of old blue serge and white silk. The full, round skirt is finished at the bottom with a deep hem; the top is gathered and joined to the body, which has a lining closely adjusted by the usual number of darts and seams. The full, low-necked front and backs are gathered near the top to form a standing frill, and droop softly over a deep, pointed girdle; the linings exposed to round-yoke depth above, are covered with yoke facings of silk. The closing is made invisibly at the center of the back. The coat sleeves have full, short puffs which spread in balloon fashion and impart a desirable broad-shouldered effect. Each wrist is trimmed with a band of white silk and a similar band decorates the skirt near the lower edge.

The simplicity of the mode will commend it to the home dressmaker for developing cashmere, vicuna, whipcord, flannel and all sorts of seasonable woolens. Velvet, faille or Bengaline will unite beautifully with any preferred variety of wool goods, and if garniture be desired, fancy braid, gimp, balloon, ribbon, etc., may be added.

Girls aged five to twelve look pretty in this frock.

6394
View Showing Dress Shirred.

No. 6406   No. 6394

6394
Front View.

6394
Back View.

6406
Front View.

6406
Back View.

1893 Girls' Dress and Guimpe

No. 6090 — This dress is portrayed made of figured challis, trimmed with baby ribbon and worn with a guimpe of white mull.

The dress may be worn with a guimpe of the same or a contrasting material, and is here shown charmingly developed in dotted cambric. The skirt is full and round and is finished at the bottom with a deep hem; the top is gathered and joined to the body, which is shaped in low, pointed outline at the top. The front and backs of the body are gathered a short distance from the upper edge to form a pretty standing frill at the top; they are arranged upon plain lining-portions and the fullness at the lower edge is drawn to the center of the front and back by two rows of shirring. The closing is made at the center of the back with buttonholes and buttons. The short puff sleeves are arranged upon smooth linings; they rise with quaint effect above the shoulders and are turned under at the lower edges and gathered to form a pretty frill finish. The waist is encircled by a wrinkled belt arranged upon a smooth lining. The ends of the belt are turned under and gathered to form pretty frills and are closed at the center of the back. If undesirable, the belt may be omitted, as shown in the small engraving.

Chambray, lawn, nainsook, percale, gingham and crépon are a few of the many fashionable fabrics that will develop attractively by the mode. All sorts of seasonable woolens are appropriate for a dress of this kind, and ribbon, feather-stitching, tucks, embroidery, frills, etc., may ornament the skirt.

This pattern has been designed to be worn by three to twelve-year-old girls.

6090
View without Belt.

6090
Front View.

6090
Back View.

1893
Girls' Dresses

No. 6370 — The dress is here portrayed made of white linen lawn and wide embroidered edging, daintily trimmed with narrow embroidered edging and feather-stitched bands. It has a full skirt which is hemmed at the bottom and gathered at the top, where it is joined to the round waist. The waist is simply shaped by underarm and shoulder seams; the closing is made at the center of the back with buttonholes and small pearl buttons. The bishop sleeves, which were always so popular for children's garments, are effectively introduced; they are gathered at the top and bottom and finished with round cuffs, which are sufficiently wide to slip comfortably over the hand. All appearance of plainness is removed from the dress by gathered bretelles of embroidered edging; they are fashionably wide over the shoulders, where they droop softly over the sleeves and are becomingly narrowed toward the ends, which are inclosed in the seam joining the waist to the skirt. The gathered edge of each bretelle is tastefully concealed by a feather-stitched band. At the neck is a rolling collar in two sections, the ends of which flare broadly at the center of the front and back; the loose edges of the collar are daintily trimmed with narrow embroidery.

This dainty little dress may be fashioned from embroidered batiste, Bulgarian flouncing, crépon, challis, chambray, gingham, dimity or printed lawn, and two-toned embroidery, appliqué bands, lace, ribbon, cotton, gimps or braids will form attractive garniture. A pretty dress may be made of pale blue nainsook, the bretelles being of the material trimmed with narrow white embroidered edging and the portions of the waist revealed between the bretelles faced with white all-over embroidery. The collar may be omitted in favor of a standing frill of embroidered edging. Another charming gown may be fashioned from cream-white China silk. The bretelles and cuffs may be made of Margot lace in a creamy shade.

Little girls from six months to seven years of age will look adorable in this costume.

No. 6370

No. 6405

6370
Front View.

6370
Back View.

6405
Front View.

6405
View Showing Low Neck.

6405
Back View.

No. 6405 — The dress is here represented made of plaid gingham and trimmed with white embroidered edging. The full, round skirt is finished at the bottom with a deep hem, gathered at the top and joined to a rather short-waisted body that is shaped with underarm and short shoulder seams and has a pretty Pompadour yoke. Three box-plaits are laid at the center of the front; in the back similar plaits are arranged, the middle plait at the back being made in the right back. The dress is closed at the center of the back with buttonholes and buttons, and at the neck is a moderately high standing collar tastefully trimmed with an upright frill of embroidered edging. The bishop sleeves are fashionably full and are gathered at the top and bottom and finished with cuffs, which are daintily trimmed at the hand with frills of embroidered edging. A stylish air is given the gown by shaped epaulette-like bretelles which are included in the seams joining the side edges of the yoke to the front and back, the free edges of the bretelles being decorated with embroidered edging. A frill of edging also follows the joining of the yoke to the body, with dainty effect. The waist may be made up with a low, square neck, as illustrated.

The mode will develop attractively in percale, chambray, embroidered batiste, linen lawn, challis, figured crépon and cashmere, and may be trimmed with all-over embroidery, lace, insertion, ribbon, fancy bands, braid, gimp, galloon, etc. A dainty dress may be made of white serge, the yoke and cuffs being trimmed with vertical rows of white soutache braid showing dashes of gold. When developed in cotton fabrics, rows of nainsook insertion may be attractively placed between the box-plaits.

This costume can be worn by girls from two to eight years old.

1893 Girls' Dress

No. 6122 — The dress may be worn with a guimpe of the same or a contrasting material and is here shown daintily developed in chambray, with embroidered edging and feather-stitched bands for decoration. The skirt reaches to a fashionable depth and is full and round. The lower edge is finished with a deep hem; the top is gathered and joined to a short-waisted body which is shaped in low, square outline at the top. The body is adjusted by shoulder and underarm seams and closed at the center of the back with buttonholes and buttons. Pretty fullness is arranged at the center of the front and at each side of the closing by gathers at the top and bottom; the gathered upper edges are finished with a feather-stitched band, above which a frill of embroidered edging rises prettily. A frill of edging and a feather-stitched band conceal the joining of the body and skirt at each side and are continued up the front over the shoulders and down the backs to outline jacket fronts and jacket backs. The short puff sleeves are very full and are gathered at the top to rise high above the shoulders; the lower edges are gathered and finished with narrow bands, that are decorated with drooping frills of embroidered edging headed by feather-stitched bands.

Plain or embroidered nainsook or chambray, percale, lawn or any preferred variety of woolen goods will develop the mode beautifully; lace, embroidery, insertion, tucks, baby ribbon or feather-stitching may supply the garniture.

This pattern was designed for girls from one to six years old.

6122

6122
Front View.

6122
Back View.

6122

1893 Girls' Empire Dress

No. 6081 — The dress is in the quaint Empire style and is here pictured made of white hemstitched nainsook and embroidered edging. The full, round skirt reaches to the ankles, falling in soft folds from the short body, to which it is joined. The body is shaped in Pompadour outline both front and back, is adjusted by shoulder and underarm seams and is closed at the center of the back with buttonholes and buttons. Broad, gathered bretelles of embroidered edging cross the shoulders, falling in picturesque fashion upon the short puff sleeves; their ends, which are narrowed to points, extend to the lower edges of the front and backs. Sections of ribbon conceal the gathered edges of the bretelles and are tied in pretty butterfly bows on the shoulders. The front and backs are decorated between the bretelles with upturning rows of embroidery. The puff sleeves are gathered at the top and bottom and are finished with narrow bands, from the lower edges of which tiny frills of embroidery droop prettily.

The guimpe, which is made of red India silk, has a full, square yoke that is turned under at the top and shirred to form a standing frill about the neck. The closing is made invisibly at the center of the back. The shirt sleeves are shirred near their lower edges to form frills about the hands.

The toilette will develop attractively in plain or embroidered batiste, nainsook, chambray or any other pretty cotton fabric; if a combination be desired, a guimpe of surah, mull or Swiss may accompany a dress of cashmere, vailing, challis, crépon, French serge or merino. Irish-point lace, velvet ribbon, feather-stitching, etc., may supply the trimming.

Pattern No. 6081 is for girls from six months to twelve years of age.

6081
Back View.

6081
Front View.

6940
Front View.

Ladies' Costume, with peplum.

6940
Side-Back View.

6940

1894
Ladies' Costume

No. 6940 — The costume displays a simplicity of construction which will adapt it especially to the various washable fabrics devoted to Summer gowns and is here depicted made of fancy-striped gingham and trimmed with white insertion. The skirt is the new four-gored style and is fashionably wide, measuring three yards and a half at the bottom in the medium sizes. The shaping of the front and side gores produces a becomingly close adjustment over the hips, the slight fullness at the top being collected in gathers; the wide back-breadth is gathered up closely at the top to fall in spreading *godets* or flute folds to the bottom. A placket is finished at the center of the back and the top of the skirt is completed with a belt. The decoration consists of three rows of insertion applied a little above the lower edge.

The waist is worn beneath the skirt and

may be made up with or without a lining that is closely adjusted by the customary darts and seams and closed at the center of the front. The fronts are disposed in becoming folds at each side of the closing, which is made invisibly at the center by gathers at the top and three short rows of shirring at the waistline. The seamless back is smooth across the shoulders and has fullness at the waistline collected in three short rows of shirring; it is separated from the fronts by underarm gores which ensure a smooth adjustment at the sides. A stylish accessory is an independent peplum which is fashioned in circular style and gathered at the center of the back to make more pronounced the rolling folds that result from the shaping. The ends of the peplum flare slightly at the center of the front; its upper edge is joined to a belt, the ends of which are closed invisibly. The full puff sleeves droop in graceful fashion to below the elbow and are arranged upon coat-shaped linings, which are covered below the puffs with

deep cuff-facings of gingham each trimmed with five spaced rows of insertion. At the neck is a close-fitting standing collar trimmed at the upper and lower edges with a row of insertion. The fronts and back are decorated at the top with three rows of similar insertion applied to outline a round yoke; three rows of similar insertion encircle the body at the bust. The lower edge and ends of the peplum are ornamented with a single row of insertion and the upper and lower edges of the belt are also trimmed with insertion.

The costume will make up daintily in silk gingham, percale, cotton crépon, dimity, lawn, nainsook, chambray and other washable fabrics, and with equally effective results in all sorts of seasonable woolens and stylish silks. Rows of washable braid or insertion may be applied to a costume of this kind developed in washable goods, and a lace-trimmed frill of the material will form a stylish foot-trimming for the skirt.

1894 Ladies' Dress

No. 6888 — The costume is shown made up for dressy afternoon wear in Summer, the materials being black and white figured silk-finished cotton foulard, white India silk and white lace edging. The skirt is fashioned in circular style, and like the majority of skirts now worn, displays fullness at the back only, a smooth effect being produced at the top of the front and sides by means of the shaping and skillfully located darts. The back is gathered at the top to fall in *godet* or funnel folds that spread in regulation fashion to the lower edge. the skirt is trimmed at the bottom, at the knee and some distance below the hips with gradu-

ated self-headed frills that are arranged with a festoon effect at the sides, where they are ornamented with butterfly bows of black moiré ribbon.

The full fronts and back of the fanciful, round body are separated by underarm gores and arranged upon a closely adjusted body lining. They are gathered at the top and the fullness at the lower edge is drawn closely by three short rows of shirring at the center of the back and at each side of the closing, which is made invisibly at the center of the front. A full seamless, round yoke that is gathered to produce a puff effect covers the upper part of the body lining and is decorated at the top and bottom with bands of insertion. A crush collar that covers the standing collar is cut from India silk to match the yoke; its frill-finished ends are closed at the center of the back. The sleeves are arranged in double puffs that reach to the

elbow, below which they droop in frills; they have smooth linings which are here cut away beneath the frills, and the puffs are topped by lace caps, which are broad on the shoulders and are narrowed considerably under the arms. A crush girdle included in the pattern is omitted in favor of a moiré ribbon girdle, the ends of which are tied in a butterfly bow at the right side.

Very picturesque costumes for afternoon or evening wear in the mountains, by the sea-shore or in town may be developed by the mode in figured India or China silk, silk crépon, satin-striped challis, or figured organdy made up over silk or sateen. All sorts of pretty woolens and stylish cottons are likewise appropriate for costumes of this kind, with garnitures of lace or embroidery.

The hat is trimmed with silk and flowers.

6888

7071 and 78074

1894 Ladies' Calling Toilette

No. 7071 and No. 7074 — This consists of a ladies' basque and skirt.

Pearl-colored crépon and black velvet were here selected for the toilette with black velvet ribbon lace insertion and silver buckles for garniture. The handsomely shaped four-gored skirt is trimmed in pointed tablier outline with a row of white lace insertion laid over black velvet ribbon; rows of black velvet ribbon radiate downward from the insertion, each row being notched at the lower end and arranged just above in a loop that is secured by a buckle.

The shapely basque is fitted in front by double bust darts and closed invisibly at the center, and the close adjustment is completed by underarm and side-back gores and a curving center seam. The fullness below the waistline is altogether the result of the shaping. The voluminous sleeves are mounted on coat-shaped linings, and each is made with an inside seam and an outside seam that extends to the elbow; extravagant fullness is collected in gathers at the top and plaits at one side edge, and additional fullness is formed into plaits above the outside seam, the result being one of the most stylish and becoming sleeves now in vogue. The wrist decoration is a pointed velvet cuff overlaid at the upper edge with lace insertion.

The velvet collar is moderately high, and extending from its lower edge at becoming intervals are rows of velvet ribbon, each of which terminates in a loop and notched end. A row of lace insertion over velvet ribbon is applied in the outline of a pointed yoke, being arranged to partly cover the loops.

Very dressy toilettes will be made up by the mode in silk and wool mixtures, serge, crépon, basket weaves, etc., and garniture will be supplied by bands of ribbon or velvet in conjunction with lace insertion.

The hat is fine French felt trimmed with silk cord and velvet ribbon.

1894 Misses' Dress

No. 6871 — The dress displays an air of quaintness and simplicity which will render it particularly appropriate for graduation or commencement exercises, and is here portrayed made of crépon and trimmed with lace insertion and ribbon. The stylishly full skirt has a straight lower edge and measures fully three yards round in the middle sizes; it is gathered at the top to fall in graceful folds from the body, to which it is joined; its lower edge is finished with a deep hem. The body is made over a high-necked body-lining closely adjusted by single bust darts and underarm and side-back gores, and has a full front and full backs, which are low and straight across at the top and are separated by underarm gores to produce a smooth adjustment at the sides. The full front and backs are drawn into pretty folds by gathers at the top; the fullness at the lower edge is collected in gathers at the center of the front and at each side of the closing, which is made invisibly at the center of the back. The visible part of the lining is faced with the material and presents the effect of a square yoke, from the lowest edges of which a deep frill droops gracefully. The frill is gathered at the top to fall with pretty fullness at the front and back and extends smoothly under the arms; its lower edge is ornamented with a band of insertion. The coat sleeves have full balloon puffs, which extend to the elbow and spread picturesquely below double sleeve-caps that are gathered to droop in soft folds on the shoulders. The ends of the sleeve caps extend to the upper edge of the frill at the front and back and the free edges of the caps are trimmed with insertion. The gathered edges of the caps are covered with twisted sections of ribbon, the ends of which disappear at the front and back beneath rosette-bows of similar ribbon. Each wrist is decorated with two encircling bands of insertion and a band of similar insertion trims the collar, which is in close-fitting standing style and becomingly high. The front and back of the dress are decorated above the frill with two bands of insertion; the waist is encircled by a ribbon sash which is prettily bowed at the center of the back, its notched ends falling low upon the skirt. The dress may be made up with or without the frill and with only one cap, as illustrated.

Attractive dresses may be developed by the mode in plain or figured India silk, crépon, dotted vailing, challis, étamine, silk-and-wool novelty goods and the numerous dainty cotton fabrics which are devoted to Summer gowns. Plain, shaded, or ombré silk or taffeta may be tastefully used in a dress of this kind in combination with any variety of woolen goods, and deep Rococo embroidery or point de Géne lace may form the caps.

6871
View without Frill and with only One Cap.

6871
Front View.

6871
Back View.

1894 Misses' Dress

No. 6912 — Very pretty effects may be achieved with thin materials made up after this mode. The dress is here represented made of white dotted Swiss and magenta velvet. It may be made with a high or a low neck and with elbow or long sleeves, as illustrated. The skirt is full and deeply hemmed at the lower edge, where it measures about two yards and a half round in the middle sizes; it is gathered at the top and falls in soft, graceful folds from the full, round waist to which it is joined. The waist has a full front and full backs shaped in low, round outline at the top and joined in underarm and shoulder seams; it is provided with a high-necked lining fitted by single bust darts and underarm and side-back gores and is closed invisibly at the center of the back. The fullness is prettily disposed at the top of the full front in four rows of shirring, the upper one being at a sufficient distance from the upper edge to form a frill finish; the fullness at the lower edge is drawn toward the center by a short row of gathers; gathers are also made at each side of the closing in the back to draw the fullness toward the center. The lining revealed above the waist with round yoke effect is faced with the Swiss, and at the neck is a close-fitting standing collar. Very full, drooping puffs that extend to the elbow are adjusted over the smooth, coat-shaped sleeves; they are gathered at the top and bottom and are tastefully topped by ripple caps of magenta velvet. The caps taper narrowly toward the ends and are deepest at the center, where they droop over the sleeves in a point; they fall in pretty, soft folds, but are perfectly smooth at the top. The waist is encircled by a girdle of velvet, which presents a pointed upper outline at the center of the front and is of belt depth at the sides and back, the ends being closed at the center of the back.

There is an air of youthfulness and grace in the appearance of this dress which insures its appreciation by those who desire to fashion dresses of dimity, lawn, batiste, Swiss or fancy silk. A trifling amount of some delicate shade of velvet will give an all-white dress a pretty touch and increase the dressiness of some materials that come in light or deep tints.

6912
Front View.

6912
Back View.

1894 Misses' Dress
(to be worn with a guimpe)

No. 6700 — The dress is simple, yet dressy in effect and will be especially admired for formal occasions made, as here represented, in cream-white China silk and trimmed with lace and a sash of ribbon that is drawn softly about the waist and tied in a bow of short loops and long ends at the back. The full skirt, which is hemmed deeply at the bottom and gathered at the top, falls in pretty folds from the full, low-necked waist, to which it is joined. It measures three yards round at the bottom in the middle sizes. The waist is arranged over a body lining fitted by single bust darts and underarm and side-back gores, and the closing is invisibly made at the center of the back. The full front and full backs are connected by underarm gores and short shoulder seams and are turned under at the top and shirred twice to form a pretty standing frill-heading, the fullness at the lower edges being collected in a short row of gathers at the center of the front and at each side of the closing. Full caps of graduated depth, the lower one reaching almost to the elbow, give becoming breadth to the shoulders and add a stylish touch; they are gathered at the top and fall with becoming fullness over the arm, their free edges being tastefully outlined with lace. A standing frill of lace trims the neck edge of the waist.

A guimpe should be worn with the dress, except on cremonious occasions, when it may be expedient to appear in full dress, in which case the low neck and short sleeves will be *de rigueur.* For best dresses China silk, fine French challis, *Henriettas* in delicate hues, and fancy figured silks will be appropriate; but for general wear, serge, cashmere, camel's-hair and novelty suitings will be serviceable and proper. Ribbon, gimp, galloon, lace or embroidery will be effective garnitures.

This is an attractive costume for eight to sixteen-year-old girls.

6912
View Showing Low Neck and Short Sleeves.

6700
Front View.

6700
Back View.

7110
Front View.

7110
Back View.

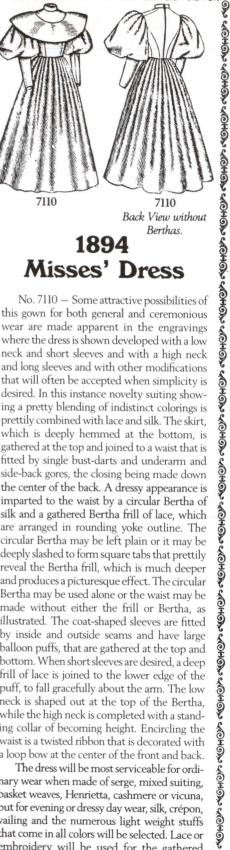

7110

7110
Back View without Berthas.

1894 Misses' Dress

No. 7110 — Some attractive possibilities of this gown for both general and ceremonious wear are made apparent in the engravings where the dress is shown developed with a low neck and short sleeves and with a high neck and long sleeves and with other modifications that will often be accepted when simplicity is desired. In this instance novelty suiting showing a pretty blending of indistinct colorings is prettily combined with lace and silk. The skirt, which is deeply hemmed at the bottom, is gathered at the top and joined to a waist that is fitted by single bust-darts and underarm and side-back gores, the closing being made down the center of the back. A dressy appearance is imparted to the waist by a circular Bertha of silk and a gathered Bertha frill of lace, which are arranged in rounding yoke outline. The circular Bertha may be left plain or it may be deeply slashed to form square tabs that prettily reveal the Bertha frill, which is much deeper and produces a picturesque effect. The circular Bertha may be used alone or the waist may be made without either the frill or Bertha, as illustrated. The coat-shaped sleeves are fitted by inside and outside seams and have large balloon puffs, that are gathered at the top and bottom. When short sleeves are desired, a deep frill of lace is joined to the lower edge of the puff, to fall gracefully about the arm. The low neck is shaped out at the top of the Bertha, while the high neck is completed with a standing collar of becoming height. Encircling the waist is a twisted ribbon that is decorated with a loop bow at the center of the front and back.

The dress will be most serviceable for ordinary wear when made of serge, mixed suiting, basket weaves, Henrietta, cashmere or vicuna, but for evening or dressy day wear, silk, crépon, vailing and the numerous light weight stuffs that come in all colors will be selected. Lace or embroidery will be used for the gathered Bertha and sleeve frills and silk or velvet, for the circular Bertha.

1894 Girls' Dress

No. 6928 — For school or home wear this dress will be a great favorite. It possesses features that are extremely becoming to growing girls. The material chosen for its present development is heliotrope suiting and the garniture is black braid. The skirt, which is the full round style, extends to a fashionable depth and is deeply hemmed at the bottom and gathered at the top, where it is joined to the body, falling in soft, graceful folds about the figure. The body has a full front and full backs and is provided with a body lining that is adjusted by single bust darts and underarm and side-back gores. The full front and backs are low and rounding at the top, the fullness being drawn by gathers at the top and bottom at the center of the front and at each side of the closing, which is made at the center of the back. The body lining is exposed in rounding outline at the top and is faced with the material trimmed at the bottom with three rows of braid. Deep bretelles having pointed ends are joined smoothly to the body and fall over the sleeves in ripples resulting from their shaping; they are stylishly decorated at their ends and lower edges with three rows of braid. Very full puffs extending to the elbows are arranged over the smooth, coat-shaped sleeves; they are gathered at the top and bottom and spread stylishly from the arm, and the wrists are trimmed with three encircling rows of braid. At the neck is a close-fitting standing collar overlaid by three encircling rows of braid. The skirt is trimmed above the hem with three rows of braid, and three rows of braid cross the full front at the bust and are continued across the back, with pretty effect. The dress may be made up without the bretelles, as illustrated.

The practical and becoming style of the dress renders it a suitable mode for silk, challis, vailing, cashmere, serge, batiste, lawn or gingham. Variation in the selection and arrangement of trimming is quite permissible, and on washable fabrics bands of insertion or lace may be used with excellent effect.

This attractive dress is for girls from three to nine years of age.

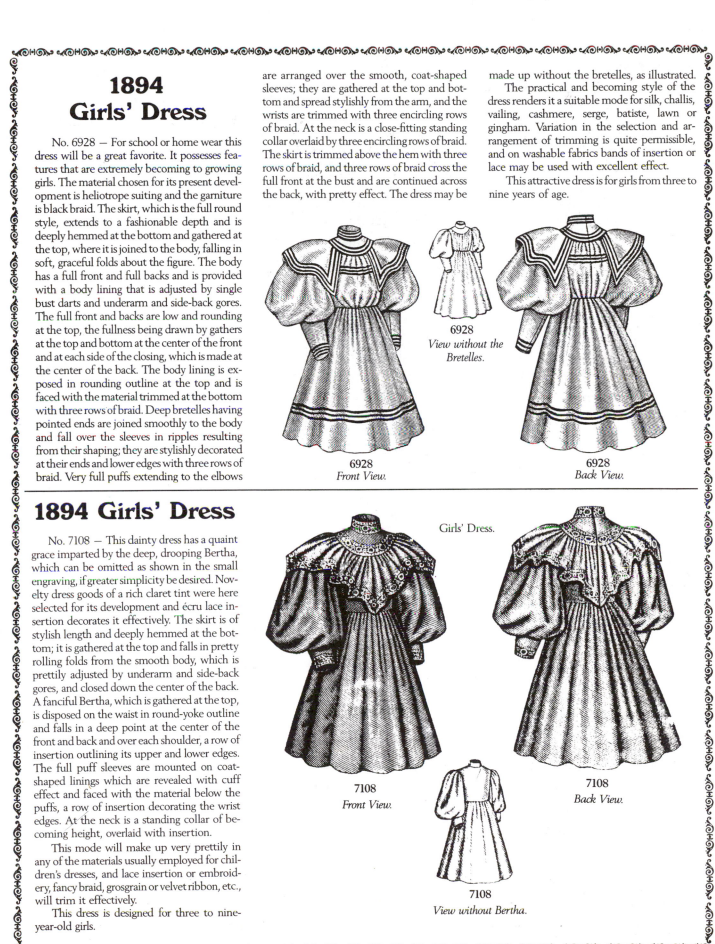

6928
View without the Bretelles.

6928
Front View.

6928
Back View.

Girls' Dress.

7108
Front View.

7108
Back View.

7108
View without Bertha.

1894 Girls' Dress

No. 7108 — This dainty dress has a quaint grace imparted by the deep, drooping Bertha, which can be omitted as shown in the small engraving, if greater simplicity be desired. Novelty dress goods of a rich claret tint were here selected for its development and écru lace insertion decorates it effectively. The skirt is of stylish length and deeply hemmed at the bottom; it is gathered at the top and falls in pretty rolling folds from the smooth body, which is prettily adjusted by underarm and side-back gores, and closed down the center of the back. A fanciful Bertha, which is gathered at the top, is disposed on the waist in round-yoke outline and falls in a deep point at the center of the front and back and over each shoulder, a row of insertion outlining its upper and lower edges. The full puff sleeves are mounted on coat-shaped linings which are revealed with cuff effect and faced with the material below the puffs, a row of insertion decorating the wrist edges. At the neck is a standing collar of becoming height, overlaid with insertion.

This mode will make up very prettily in any of the materials usually employed for children's dresses, and lace insertion or embroidery, fancy braid, grosgrain or velvet ribbon, etc., will trim it effectively.

This dress is designed for three to nine-year-old girls.

1894 Girls' Dress

No. 6684 — The dress is here represented made of cardinal red crépon and black silk. The skirt, which is in the full, round style, is deeply hemmed at the bottom and falls in pretty folds from gathers at the top, where it is joined to the body. The smooth front and backs are separated by underarm gores and shaped in low pointed outline at the top; they are disposed over a high-necked lining and the closing is made invisibly at the center of the back. Arranged upon the upper part of the lining is a full, seamless yoke, which is gathered at the bottom and turned under at the top and shirred far enough from the upper edge to form a standing frill. The sleeves are in mutton-leg style and are fashionably full at the top; they are shaped by inside and outside seams and mounted on coat-shaped linings. Below the elbow a close adjustment is maintained and the wrists are plainly completed.

When the dress is made up for school or ordinary wear the standard cashmeres, serges or Henriettas in such colors as are serviceable yet becoming to growing girls will be the most satisfactory selections. For dressy wear, India silk, challis, crépon, hopsackings in changeable effects, wide-wale serges and fancy mohair effects in silk and wool will make up attractively.

This is an attractive costume for girls from three to nine years old.

6684
Front View.

6684
Back View.

1894 Girls' Apron

No. 6693 — The apron combines beauty and utility, and as it is certainly protective, it will be especially adapted for school and play wear. It is here pictured made of white cross-barred cambric and trimmed with embroidered edging. It consists of a full front and full backs joined by underarm and short shoulder seams and is gathered at the top to fall with pretty fullness at the center from a pointed yoke, which is smoothly fitted by seams on the shoulders. The closing is made to a desirable depth at the center of the back with buttonholes and buttons. The bishop sleeves are a pleasing feature of the apron; they are gathered at the top and bottom and are finished with round cuffs daintily trimmed at the wrists with a frill of narrow embroidered edging. A fanciful air is produced by the addition of Bertha-bretelles, which are included in the seams joining the apron to the yoke. The bretelles are made with a seam at the front and are of great width

on the shoulders, where they are gathered; they are becomingly narrowed at the center of the front and back; their ends flare broadly. The lower edge of the bretelles is decorated with embroidered edging and a standing frill of similar edging forms a becoming neck completion. Included in the side seams at the waistline are the plaited ends of narrow ties, which are bowed at the back. The free ends of the ties are hemmed, and the bottom of the apron is finished with a deep hem-facing of the material.

Very dainty aprons are made of dimity, lawn, Swiss, organdy or fine French mull, nainsook and fancy tucking, lace insertion, fine embroidery and fancy bands affording attractive garniture. The yoke and cuffs may be made of tucking, all-over embroidery, or alternate rows of insertion or tucking. For general wear gingham, chambray or figured batiste decorated with two-toned embroidery will prove serviceable.

This apron is appropriately worn by two to ten-year-old girls.

6693

1894
Girls' Toilette

(to be worn with a guimpe)

6693
View without Bretelles.

6693
Front View.

6693
Little Girls' Apron.

No. 6692 — Canary cashmere was here selected for making the dress, which is particularly becoming to wee women, the flounce sleeves and Bertha frill giving it that picturesque air which is counted so desirable a feature in little girls' attire. The full, round skirt is deeply hemmed at the bottom and is gathered at the top and joined with graceful fullness to the very short-waisted body. The body is shaped in low, round outline at the top and is made with underarm and short shoulder seams, and the closing is performed invisibly at the center of the back. From the neck edge falls a deep Bertha-frill of cashmere that is tastefully trimmed at the lower edge with three rows of bébé ribbon. The full flounce sleeves give breadth to the shoulders and the free edge of each is trimmed with three rows of bébé ribbon.

The guimpe is made of white India silk. It has a full, square yoke arranged upon a front and backs that are joined in shoulder and underarm seams and closed at the center of the back. The yoke is turned under at the top to form a standing frill about the neck, and the guimpe is drawn in to the figure at the waistline by means of tapes inserted in a casing. The full sleeves are drawn by rows of shirring near their lower edges to form frills about the hands.

Plain and figured India silk, taffeta, silk-and-wool crépon, satin-striped challis, gingham, embroidered vailing, dimity, embroidered flouncing and batiste will make charming dresses of this kind, and lace, insertion or fine embroidered edging will supply pretty decoration. The guimpe may be made of crêpe de Chine or net.

Girls from two to eight years of age wear this costume prettily.

6692
View without Bertha Frill.

6692
Front View.

6692
Back View.

1895 Ladies' Tea Gown

No. 7427 — The tea gown possesses an elegance of outline and a gracefulness that are unsurpassed; its attractive features are here pleasingly emphasized by the combination of black *gros de Londres*, turquoise-blue silk and deep *beurre*-yellow lace edging. The front opens from the shoulders upon a full vest, which falls in flowing folds from gathers at the top over closely adjusted Princess fronts of lining that close at the center to a desirable depth and are tacked together below. The full vest is trimmed at the bust with two rows of ribbon that outline points at the center beneath knotted kerchief ends of similar ribbon; at the bottom is applied a frill of *beurre*-yellow lace edging headed by two bands of ribbon with a band of *beurre*-yellow insertion between them, the bands of ribbon being decorated at intervals with kerchief ends to match those at the bust.

Long ties of similar ribbon confine the fullness at the waistline, being attached underneath the fronts and knotted at the center, where their long, notched ends fall low upon the skirt. The fronts fall free from the shoulder seam, where they are each laid in a broad box-plait, which overlaps the hemmed front edge with the effect of double folds and maintains its folds to below the waistline, spreading into soft folds below. The fronts are curved gracefully to the figure at the side by long underarm darts taken up with the corresponding darts in the Princess fronts of lining. The back is in Princess style and is adjusted by the customary gores and curving center seam, the shaping of the skirt portion producing a series of stately flutes or *godets* that spread into the train, which is of graceful length, but may be cut off if not liked, the pattern also providing for a gown of round length. A deep Bertha of lace falls in full, soft folds at the back and over the shoulders; its ends pass beneath the box-plaits in the front. The sleeves have huge balloon puffs which

reach to the elbow and droop with old-time quaintness from beneath the Bertha and are trimmed below the puffs with three encircling rows of insertion. At the neck is a standing collar decorated with a wrinkled black ribbon, the ends of which are concealed by a rosette-bow of similar ribbon.

The range of fabrics adapted to a gown of this kind is so wide that all tastes and purses may be suited in its fashioning. It will make up as appropriately in challis, cashmere, foulé and other simple woolens as in such stately fabrics as *gros de Tours, peau de cygne*, grosgrain silk and taffeta. The full vest will usually contrast in hue or texture with the remainder of the gown; for garniture, any pretty variety of rich or inexpensive lace, insertion, galloon, gimp, fancy braid, ribbon or feather-stitching done with heavy rope silk or Roman floss will be pretty and effective. The pattern also provides for elbow sleeves, in which case the sleeves will be finished with deep frills. The gown may be made less elaborate by omitting the Bertha.

No. 7427.

7427
Side-Front View.

7427
Side-Back View.

7427
View without Bertha.

1895
Ladies' Costume

No. 7424 — The dressy costume is here shown made up in plain and figured silk, velvet and lace, the figured silk having a yellow-brown ground strewn with darker figures, and the plain silk, which composes the vest, being lighter in hue than the ground. The waist lining is well fitted by double bust darts and the usual seams and closed at the center of the front, and it supports the full vest, which is gathered at the neck and shirred at the lower edge, where it droops in blouse fashion over a velvet belt-section. A novel and very artistic effect is contributed by loose jacket-fronts that lap over white lace jabots arranged to droop with charming grace over the full vest; underarm gores separate the jacket fronts from the seamless back, which has a box-plait down the center graduated narrow toward the lower edge. At the neck is a standing collar covered with a crush collar of velvet, the frill-finished ends of which are fastened at the back. The deep cape-collar of velvet is in two parts with square ends that flare stylishly at the front and back; its free edges are tastefully decorated with lace Vandykes.

Bouffant leg-o'-mutton sleeves shaped by one seam only are mounted on coat-shaped linings and stand out broadly at the top where the fullness is collected in gathers that cause the material to break into soft wrinkles and folds to the elbow, below which the adjustment is stylishly close.

The skirt possesses the grace that is noticeable in all of this season's modes and has a pleasing though not an excessive flare at the bottom. It fits the figure closely at the top of the front and sides, and considerable fullness is arranged at the back, where three *godets* are formed. The *godets* are lined throughout with hair-cloth and spread downward and outward in flute-like folds to the lower edge. A narrow facing of hair-cloth is added to the other gores to emphasize the flare.

Very effective and very fashionable costumes may be made up after this mode in faced cloth, camel's-hair, zibeline or any of the pretty crépons, and more elaborate gowns may be developed in *gros de Lóndres*, brocaded silk or velvet. Many lovely combinations may be effected by this design. Thus, a gown of dark plum-colored cloth may have an old-rose vest, and ivory-white lace for the jabots, while a collar of rich plum-colored velvet decorated with lace Vandykes will be highly ornamental. Green cloth with a blue or yellow fabric for the vest and silver gray with pink are equally stylish.

The hat is trimmed with ribbon, lace and jet.

No. 7424.

7424
View without Jabots and Crush Collar.

7424
Side-Front View.

7424
Side-Back View.

1895
Misses' Costume

No. 7875 — Finely woven camel's hair in a pretty blue shade is here combined with batiste and batiste insertion. The fronts have stylish fullness disposed in a double box-plait over the closing and in gathers at the neck and waistline and droop slightly in French blouse fashion at the center. The lining is fitted by single bust darts and the usual seams and underarm gores connect the full fronts with the seamless back, which has fullness closely plaited at the bottom. A stylish feature is the sailor collar with broad square ends extending to the bust; the collar is made of strips of batiste alternating with rows of insertion. Its outer edge is finished with a frill of batiste embroidered edging. The standing collar is covered with a wrinkled stock having frill-finished ends which close at the back. The one-seam leg-of-mutton sleeves have ample fullness at the top and fit closely on the forearm. Ribbon frames the fullness at the center of the front and ends in a long loop at each side below the softly wrinkled belt.

The six-gored skirt has a stylish flare at the bottom and graceful fullness forming three godets at the back, the front and sides fitting smoothly at the top.

Serge, cheviot, novelty suiting and various standard weaves like cashmere will make up admirably by the mode. Embroidery, braid or passementerie will decorate it effectively.

This design is appropriate for misses from ten to sixteen years of age.

No. 7875.

7875
Front View.

7875
Back View.

7875
*View without Sailor Collar
and Crush Collar.*

Misses' 1895 Dress

No. 7867 — Striped taffeta silk and plain mousseline de soie are here combined in the dress; lace ruching and ribbon decorate it becomingly. The pattern provides for a high or low neck and for long or elbow sleeves. Its present development in a low neck and elbow sleeves suggests festivities. The pretty waist of mousseline de soie is made over a fitted lining. It has gathered fullness at the lower edge drawn well to the center both front and back; underarm gores render it smooth fitting at the sides. Coat-shaped linings sustain the one-seam leg-of-mutton sleeves which spread bouffantly at the top, the elbow completion showing a softly twisted ribbon bowed at the seam. A novel accessory is the Bertha ornament which lies smoothly about the square neck. It shapes two broad fancy tabs at the front and back, is prettily curved over the shoulders and is decorated at all its edges and midway between the neck and lower edges with lace ruching. A softly twisted ribbon encircles the waist and is tied in two ends at each side of the front. The four-gored skirt is jointed to the waist and has only enough fullness at the top across the front and sides to fit gracefully, but breaks naturally into stylish soft ripples below the hips. Knotted ends of ribbon are placed at intervals over the side-front seams of the skirt and two rows of lace ruching ornament the bottom of the skirt.

The popular features that are embodied in this dress will appear to good advantage when developed in the beautiful changeable silks and soft chiffon or Liberty satin if the mode is intended for ceremonious ware. Ribbon or lace will trim it effectively. For everyday wear, serge, cashmere and various novelty goods will be chosen and braid, ribbon or lace bands or passementerie will provide decoration.

This pattern is designed to be worn by misses from ten to sixteen years old.

7867

7867
Front View.

7867
Back View.

1895 Misses' Costume

No. 7828 — A charming combination of novelty suiting, velvet and silk is here arranged in the costume. The waist is smooth, single bust darts and underarm gores fitting it at the front and sides, while a lining fitted by curved back edges and side-back gores gives a pretty shape to the wide back, which is closed at the center. A deep, pointed yoke covers the upper part of the front and an applied box-plait of velvet extends the entire length of the waist at the center of the front and back, a shorter applied plait of velvet reaching from the lower edge of the yoke to the bottom of the waist at each side of the front. The one-seam leg-o'-mutton sleeves, which are placed over coat-shaped linings, give the fashionable broad-shouldered effect and are close below the elbow. A dressy touch is given by a stock collar of silk that covers the standing collar and closes under a bow of velvet and ribbon at the back, a twist of silk and velvet outlining its upper and lower edge. A larger twist of silk and velvet follows the lower edge of the waist and terminates under a bow of velvet and ribbon at the back.

The skirt has a circular front which is dartless and smooth at the top and falls in ripples below the hips and three godets that are each laid in a box-plait at the top. The godets expand gradually toward the lower edge, where the skirt measures a little over three yards and a fourth in the middle sizes, and are held in position by an elastic strap tacked across them near the top. The placket is finished at the seam nearest the center of the back at the left side and the skirt is completed by a belt.

New silk-and-wool blendings will be chosen for this costume, with velvet of a darker shade and silk of lighter hue in combination. Scotch cheviots with rough surfaces and in checks or solid tones, heather mixtures, silk, serge and various novelty goods will make up stylishly in conjunction with velvet or contrasting dress goods.

This is an attractive costume for misses from ten to sixteen years of age.

Pattern 7828

7828
Front View.

7828
Back View.

1895 Girls' Dress

No. 7566 — The simplicity which good taste requires is an attractive feature of this picturesque dress, which is here shown made of figured challis and trimmed with ribbon in two widths. The dress has a full, straight skirt that is deeply hemmed at the bottom and gathered at the top to fall in full, soft folds from the body, which has a lining fitted by single bust darts and the usual underarm and side-back gores. The front of the body is gathered at the top and bottom and droops in pronounced blouse fashion at the center over the skirt; it is separated by underarm gores from the full backs which are arranged in soft folds by gathers at the top and bottom. The fullness at the back and front is drawn well to the center and the body is closed at the center with buttonholes and buttons. The coat sleeves have full drooping puffs which reach to the elbow; the puffs are gathered at the top and bottom, and the wrists are trimmed with three rows of narrow ribbon. A quaint feature of the dress is the bretelles, which droop in a deep point upon each sleeve and form a deep point at the front and back of the arm; they cross the shoulders smoothly and are trimmed at their free edges with three bands of narrow ribbon, their upper edges being followed with a wrinkled band of wider ribbon, the ends of which are finished with rosette bows of similar ribbon. The standing collar, which closes at the back, is covered by a wrinkled ribbon, over the ends of which a spreading bow formed of loops of ribbon is arranged. The decoration is completed by a rosette bow of ribbon tacked to the bottom of the waist at each side of the fullness in the front. The dress may be made up without the bretelles, as shown in the small view.

The little dress will make up exquisitely in cashmere, serge, foulé, camel's-hair, etc., and will be appropriately used for developing plain and embroidered chambray, spotted, striped or figured percale, embroidered flouncing, nainsook and other stylish cottons.

This pattern is designed to be worn by five to twelve-year-old girls.

7566
Girls' Dress.

7566

7566
Front View.

7566
Back View.

1895 Girls' Dress

No. 7567 — The dress, which may be daintily developed for a party gown, is here shown made up in spotted challis with lace edging and velvet rosettes for garniture. The skirt, which is full and straight, is deeply hemmed at the bottom and is gathered at the top and joined to the body, falling in full soft folds all round. The body, which is shaped in low, round outline at the top, has a full front and full backs separated by underarm gores and disposed in soft folds upon a smooth body-lining by gathers at the top and bottom, the fullness at the front drooping in blouse fashion upon the skirt. The body lining is fitted by single bust darts and underarm and side-back gores, and the dress is closed invisibly at the center of the back. The puff sleeves extend to the elbow and are mounted upon smooth linings; they are gathered at the top and bottom and spread in picturesque balloon fashion, the quaint droop on the shoulder being emphasized by the deep points of the Bertha which rest upon them. The Bertha falls smoothly from the upper edge of the body. The upper and lower edges of the Bertha are decorated with narrow point de Géne lace edging; a velvet rosette trims the bottom of the front at each side of the fullness.

The dress is suitable for the pretty silks which are used for girls' best dresses and for the numerous woolens and silk-and-wool novelties that are used for every-day or school gowns.

This dress is suitable for girls from five to twelve years old.

7567
Front View.

7567
Back View.

7567

1895
Girls' Costume

No. 7864 — Tan cashmere was here selected to make the dress, and ribbon, buttons and insertion decorate it attractively. The front of the body droops in pretty French blouse style and an ornamental effect is attained at the center by the disposal of the fullness, which is arranged in a double box-plait at the top and in gathers at the bottom. At each side of the closing the back is laid in a box-plait and under-arm gores connect the backs with the front and produce a smooth adjustment at the sides. The waist is provided with a lining fitted by single bust darts and the usual seams. The one-seam leg-o'-mutton sleeves are fashionably full above the elbow and close-fitting below and are completed by two encircling rows of ribbon overlaid with insertion. The standing collar is concealed by a softly wrinkled stock of ribbon arranged in loops at the sides. Curved rows of ribbon overlaid with insertion decorate the upper part of the front at each side of the double box-plait and three fancy buttons ornament the plait near the top. A ribbon belt encircles the waist and a full bow is tacked to it at each side of the fullness. The skirt is straight at its lower edge, which is deeply hemmed; at the top it is gathered and sewed to the waist.

The dress will be a favorite for best or ordinary wear, according to the materials of which it is made. Novelty suiting, mohair, plain or fancy cheviot, serge and, for special occasions, silks are among the fabrics that will appeal to many, and the decoration may be braid, insertion over silk or ribbon, or bands of gimp or passementerie.

Girls from five to twelve years old look pretty in this costume.

No. 7864

1895 Girls' Dress

No. 7545 — Simplicity and good style are charmingly united in the pretty little dress here shown developed in pink and white striped zephyr gingham and trimmed with narrow white embroidery and pink ribbon. The full skirt is finished at the bottom with a deep hem and is gathered at the top and joined to the body, falling in pretty folds all round. The front of the body is arranged in a broad box-plait at the center; the back displays a similar box-plait over the closing, which is made with hooks and eyes at the center. The front and backs are separated by underarm gores to insure a smooth adjustment at the sides; the body is provided with a lining snugly adjusted by the usual darts and seams. The one-seam mutton-leg sleeves, which are mounted upon smooth, coat-shaped linings, display fashionable fullness at the top and are gathered to droop in quaint style at the shoulders. They follow the outline of the forearm with comfortable closeness and are trimmed with embroidered edging applied to simulate deep, pointed cuffs. The box-plait at the front is decorated with similar edging and so also is the rolling collar, which is in two sections with widely flaring ends. The belt provided by the pattern is omitted in favor of a ribbon sash that is tied at the back in a pretty bow with long notched ends.

For the host of pretty cottons that are to be devoted to girls' summer gowns this dress is a specially attractive mode: it will also make up beautifully in Fayetta, challis, cashmere, etc., with velvet ribbon, fancy braid, gimp or feather-stitching for trimming. Plain, checked and striped piqué and *plissé* and silk gingham are washable materials that will be favored for the mode.

Girls from two to twelve years of age appropriately wear this dress.

7545

7545
Front View.

7545
Back View.

1895
Childs' Costume

No. 7553 — Buff-colored lawn and all-over embroidery are here pictured in the little dress, which is prettily decorated with ribbon, edging and fancy-stitched bands. The dress is deeply hemmed at the bottom, the hem being headed by a fancy-stitched band; it is gathered at the top and attached to a V-shaped yoke of all-over embroidery shaped by shoulder seams and closed at the back. Included in the seam joining the yoke is a Bertha-ruffle of lawn, and above it is secured a second ruffle; both ruffles are decorated at their free edges with a fancy-stitched band. The full sleeves are gathered at the top and bottom and completed with wristbands of all-over embroidery decorated with a frill of edging. The neck is finished with a standing and a falling frill of edging; the yoke is outlined with ribbon which is prettily tied at the point of the yoke in a full bow having long, flowing ends.

So charmingly simple a mode as this will find many admirers, and the assortment of materials suitable for its development includes China and India silk, fine nainsook, lawn, dimity, organdy, gazine, mull, dotted Swiss, and for ordinary wear, gingham and cambric. Ribbon is at this season offered in every width and color likely to be desired for gowns of this description and velvet ribbon is fully as popular as satin. Frequently bands of lace insertion or embroidery will be used instead of the fancy-stitched bands.

This is an appropriate dress for a little girl from one to seven years old.

7553
View without Bretelles.

7553
Front View.

7553
Back View.

1895
Childs' Dress

No. 7826 — A little brunette would look charming in the dress as here developed, the materials being pale yellow cashmere figured with brown, and brown silk. The full waist is arranged over a smooth lining. Its fullness is drawn well to the center of the front and back by gathers at the top and bottom. The fullness is framed prettily by silk-lined bretelles that are each in two sections that taper narrowly at the waistline and are folded over on the shoulders in revers. Small gilt buttons decorate the long edges of the revers. The full gathered skirt is jointed to the waist. The puff sleeves are placed over coat-shaped linings that are faced with silk below the sleeves to have the effect of cuffs. A bow of ribbon is placed at the bottom of the waist between the ends of the bretelles and a bow is perched daintily on each shoulder. The standing collar is of silk.

The mode will be of great value to those who demand simplicity coupled with a dressy effect. Cashmere, camel's hair, novelty goods and materials of like weight and weave should be chosen. A little blonde may have a pale pink, blue or rose-colored cashmere relieved by ribbon bows and fancy buttons as illustrated while the warmer hues will be developed for brunettes.

Pattern No. 7826 is appropriate for children from one to seven years old.

No. 7826

7826
View without Bretelles.

7826
Front View.

7826
Back View.

1895 Girls' Dress

No. 7561 — Pink hemstitched chambray flouncing was here chosen to make the little dress and ribbon decorates it simply but prettily. The mode is a generally becoming one and will be found very easy of development, as the short waist is simply shaped by shoulder and underarm seams and closed at the back. The flouncing is cut with the hemstitching running vertically in the waist. The full skirt is gathered at the top and sewed to the waist, falling in pretty folds about the figure; the hemstitching appears in three encircling rows above a moderately deep hem. The full sleeves are gathered at the top and bottom and completed with wristbands showing hemstitching. Bretelles cross the shoulders, starting from the lower edge of the waist in front and terminating at a corresponding depth at the back; they are gathered at the top and have hemstitched hems at their ends and lower edges; the upper edge of each is concealed by a wrinkled ribbon, the ends of which are covered by a bow placed at the center of the front and back. The standing collar is closed at the back and is encircled by a ribbon that is secured at the left side under a dainty little bow. Single bretelles are provided by the pattern and may be used with elaborate effect.

Charming little dresses, both child-like and inexpensive, will be made up after this mode in China silk, fine nainsook, dimity, batiste, lawn or the pin-dotted challies that have cream-white grounds; a trifling amount of satin or velvet ribbon will provide attractive and appropriate decoration. For best wear finely hem-stitched nainsook or chambray flouncing may be selected, the hemstitching being dressy and effective.

This dress can be worn by girls from one to eight years old.

7561
Front View.

7561
Back View.

7561
View without Frills.

1896 Ladies' Evening Dress

No. 8343 — Taffeta silk of a delicate lilac hue, white lace net and plain and embroidered white chiffon are combined in this handsome dress, striped ribbon and garlands of flowers providing the decoration. The charmingly youthful waist is gathered at the top and bottom of the front and back and underarm gores render it smooth at the sides. It is closed invisibly at the center of the front and from the round neck falls a Bertha collar that is in square yoke shape at the bottom and is closed on the left shoulder. Epaulette frills of embroidered chiffon droop over the elbow puff-sleeves which are of plain chiffon over silk and are completed by deep, pointed cuffs overlaid with lace net. Buds, blossoms and leaves compose the floral garniture that extends down the front and back in bretelle fashion and ends under a wrinkled striped ribbon artistically bowed at the left side, the long ends of the ribbon falling low over the straight, full skirt.

The full skirt flares over a five-gored skirt that will usually be stiffened at the bottom with hair-cloth, canvas or other material. The five-gored skirt may be omitted or it may be used instead of the full skirt if preferred.

There is a fascinating air of originality and youthfulness in the dress, which as here shown is suggestive of receptions, dinners, garden parties and evening dances. Lustrous taffetas or failles, and sheer organdy or mull over silk are commended as its most attractive development for youthful wear, while rich *poult de soie* or silks in Dresden or Persian coloring are approved when it is chosen by matrons.

1896 Ladies' Empire Dress

No. 8330 — This dress is most elegant and picturesque for dinner and evening wear and is shown in a combination of fancy silk having a nasturtium yellow ground figured in green and dark green brocaded silk, bead and jeweled passementerie contributing a brilliant decorative touch. The quaint, short waist, which is provided with a well-fitted lining, has a full back and full fronts gathered at the top and bottom and is closed at the front. Drooping over the sleeves and waist is a deep pointed Bertha in two sections that is bordered with narrow black passementerie. The low round neck is followed by a band of jeweled passementerie and a similar band covers the belt. A band of the jeweled passementerie is adjusted about the neck. The handkerchief cuffs are attractive features of the short puff sleeves; they are edged with beaded passementerie and flare stylishly, the corners being lightly tacked to the puffs. The belt connects the skirt and waist and laps to the left side where the placket is made. The skirt has three gores and is gathered at the top all round. A graceful Watteau laps over the waist to the neck and is inserted between the back edges of the back gores to the edge of the stylish train. If desired, the dress may be in round length and may have a high neck and full length sleeves.

1896 Ladies' Afternoon Gown

No. 8607 — This is a charming gown for afternoon wear. the present combination of plain and polka-dotted blue silk and white lace over white satin produces a very pleasing result. The fanciful waist is made with a closely-fitted lining and its perfectly smooth whole back is bias. The full fronts flare toward the middle of the shoulders over a smooth plastron and about the lower part of the waist is a wrinkled girdle that is drawn out to be deepest at the front, where its frilled ends are closed. The close-fitting sleeves are made fanciful by short bouffant puffs at the top and by deep frill caps that stand out stylishly over the puffs. A wrinkled ribbon about the bottom of the collar is knotted at the front and bowed at the back; a bow of similar ribbon is tacked to the girdle at the left side. Jet beading and lace points and insertions are effective as decoration.

Long lace points are placed on the side-front seams of the skirt, which is in five gores. The skirt spreads broadly at the front and flutes deeply at the sides and is gathered at the back.

Less elaborate costumes will be made up in combinations of woolen goods and silk. Much simplicity may be attained by making the back in the ordinary fitted style and omitting the girdle and frill caps.

1896 Misses' Visiting Costume

No. 8536 — French dimity in a pretty pink hue is here pictured in the costume and insertion, ribbon and lace edging provide the attractive decoration. The waist is made over a closely-fitted, high-necked lining and is closed at the back. The full front and backs are separated by underarm gores and the front droops slightly at the center; above the full front and backs the lining is faced with the material and the waist is decorated with insertion, lace edging and narrow ribbon to have the effect of a square yoke. Smooth sleeve-caps, slashed at the center to form two broad tabs, droop over the tops of the three-quarter length puff-sleeves which are completed with deep frills of the material, the caps and frills being decorated to correspond. The collar is encircled by a wide ribbon bowed stylishly at the back and the waist is surrounded by a wide ribbon that is bowed prettily at the side.

The seven-gored skirt is gathered at the back and flares broadly at the bottom, where it is trimmed with a lace-edged ruffle of the material headed by rows of narrow ribbon.

Ingenuity in the arrangement of decoration may have full play upon dresses made like this or organdy, lawn, challis, etc., such decorations including lace edgings, pretty ribbons and insertions.

The straw hat is trimmed with flowers and ribbon.

Misses, ages ten to sixteen, look attractive in this costume.

8536
Front View.

8536
Back View.

8536

1896
Misses' Costume

No. 8519 — The dress is very fanciful in effect and is here portrayed made up in white Swiss. The straight, full skirt is gathered, the upper edge joined to the lower edge of a notably pretty round waist. Three rows of insertion trim the skirt above its deep hem. The waist is made over a lining fitted by single bust darts and underarm and side-back gores and is closed at the back. The full front and full backs, which are joined in shoulder and underarm seams, are gathered at the upper and lower edges and ornamentally drawn in double rows of shirring along the shoulder seams and at square yoke depth across the back, and in three double rows of shirrings that are curved upward across the bust and continued diagonally under the arms and across the bottom of the back with a decidedly novel effect, the fullness standing out quaintly in a puff below the shirrings in front. The sleeves are gathered at the top and drawn close by three double rows of shirring below the elbow; they are made on coat-shaped linings and may be finished with a close cuff effect at the wrists or may extend only to three-quarter length, as preferred. In the three-quarter length the sleeves are finished with frills of lace drawn up closely at the inside of the arm. The collar is in standing style and over it is a wrinkled ribbon bowed at the back. A similar ribbon is passed about the waist and formed in a double loop-bow at the back, and the decoration is completed by a row of insertion over each double row of shirring. The material is cut away from beneath all the insertion, giving an airy, dainty effect.

The dress is suitable for soft foulard and China silks, as well as for mull, nainsook, linen batiste, dimity, lawn and organdy. Only a simple trimming should be added, the shirrings making the mode decorative in itself.

It can be worn by girls from ten to sixteen years old.

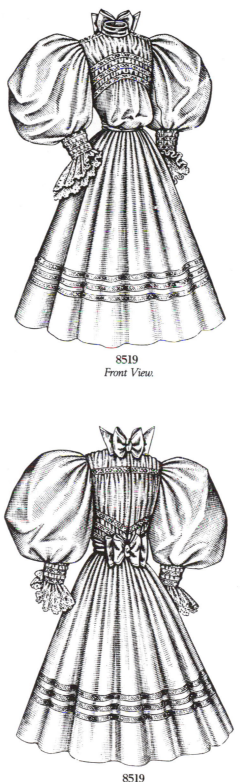

8519
Front View.

8519

8519
Back View.

1896 Girls' Dress

No. 8520 — The dress may be worn with or without a guimpe and is here made up of pink crépon with insertion, edging and ribbon bows for decoration. It is exceedingly pretty for party wear. The full gathered skirt hangs in soft folds from the body, which is simply shaped by shoulder and underarm seams and closed at the back. Drooping from the low round neck is a deep Bertha frill of the material prettily decorated with insertion and edging and the short puff-sleeves are daintily completed with bands that are overlaid with insertion, a frill of embroidered edging falling from the band. A pretty bow of ribbon is placed on the lower part of the front at each side of the center.

Pretty dresses may be made up in this way of pure white organdy, mull or nainsook and for party wear, delicate colors in the same goods may be selected. For more practical purposes, cashmere, veiling, étamine, etc., are commended. With all these fabrics, lace insertion and edging with ribbon will prove a pleasing decoration.

This design looks attractive on girls from three to twelve years old.

8520
Front View.

8520
Back View.

1896 Girls' Party Dress

No. 8521 — Figured organdy was here used for the dainty dress and frills of lace give a beautifying touch to the bretelles. The dress may have a high or square neck, as preferred. It is made with a body lining that is fitted by shoulder and underarm seams and, in the high neck, the lining is faced to have the appearance of a square yoke and finished with a standing collar. The dress portion is shaped with only short shoulder seams and is in Pompadour outline at the neck, where it is turned under and shirred twice across the front and back to form a frill heading. The sleeves may be in full length or in short puffs, the puffs being arranged on coat-shaped sleeves. Fancy bretelles cross the shoulders, their ends falling free below the square neck at the front and back.

Silk, challis, batiste, grass linen, dimity and lawn are among the materials that are suited for this dress.

Little girls from two to ten years old will look attractive in this dress.

8521

8521
Front View.

8521
Back View.

1896 Girls' Dress

No. 8529 — Very dainty and summery is the dress in its present development, which unites fancy tucking and pink lawn. The gathered skirt is deeply hemmed at the bottom and joined to a belt that finishes the lower edge of the body, which is closed at the back. A square yoke of fancy tucking forms the upper part of the body and to it are joined the full front and backs, which are drawn in soft folds by gathers at their upper and lower edges. The full bishop sleeves stand out picturesquely above their narrow wristbands. Olive-green satin ribbon is associated with wide beading, narrow edging and fancy-stitched bands in the trimming, which is child-like and attractive.

The pretty fullness of the dress will suggest its development in Swiss, lawn, organdy and soft silks, which may be plain or strewn with dainty blossoms. The garniture should consist of fine laces and ribbons in some fancy variety.

This is an appropriate dress for one to eight-year-old girls.

8529
Front View.

8529
Back View.

1896 Girls' Dress

No. 8534 — The dress is here pictured made of white lawn and trimmed with lace edging and insertion. It is shaped by shoulder seams and has a round neck filled in with a shallow round yoke; it is gathered at the front and back nearly to the shoulders, and in the seam joining it to the yoke is included a pretty handkerchief Bertha that is gathered at the top, the corners falling at the front and back of the sleeves. The dress is deeply hemmed at the bottom and closed invisibly at the back. The neck is finished with a standing frill of lace set on under a narrow band of the material. The sleeves are in bishop style and may be made with or without coat-shaped linings. When made with the linings, they are finished with cuff effect, but if without, they are finished with wristbands trimmed with insertion and edged with lace. The small view shows the dress without the Bertha.

A very charming little dress was made up in this way of grass linen trimmed with batiste edging and insertion of an openwork design, with apple-green satin ribbon underlying the insertion and showing through it with pretty effect. Dimity, organdy, lawn, batiste and challis are much in favor for dresses of this style

8534
Front View.

8534
Back View.

8534

and embroidered or lace edging and insertion in beautiful designs are now obtainable for trimming them.

This pattern was designed for girls six months to six years old.

1896 Girls' Pinafore Dress

No. 8496 — The simple construction and pleasing outlines of this dress make it an excellent style for general wear. A combination of blue and white India silk is pictured in the dress. Underarm and short shoulder seams form the shaping of the dress and the neck is in Pompadour outline. Gathers across the neck throw the fullness into pretty folds, both front and back, and the closing is made at the back with a button and buttonhole. A cording gives a decorative finish to the arms'-eyes and neck, the neck being further ornamented with a doubled frill of the material.

A pretty guimpe appears with yoke effect above the dress. The guimpe is fitted by single bust darts and underarm and side-back gores and is closed at the back. On the guimpe is arranged a full yoke that is shaped with shoulder and short underarm seams and turned under and shirred to form a standing frill at the neck, gathers collecting the fullness at the lower edge. The guimpe is completed by full sleeves that are made on coat-shaped linings and gathered at the top and bottom and finished with round cuffs.

In this dress the guimpe will usually be made of silk or mull, while the remainder of the dress will be of cashmere, crépon or some

8496
Front View.

8496
Back View.

8496

8496

other soft woolen fabric. Party dresses like this will be lavishly trimmed with lace and ribbon and are worn by girls from three to nine years old.

1897 Ladies' House Gown

No. 9010 — In this instance the gown is pictured made up in a charming combination of figured green moiré and black and white faille Princesse. The black silk is covered with jet bead trimming and is used for the fancy notched revers which are joined to the side-fronts and shape a tab on each shoulder. The side-fronts open all the way over a full flowing front and are shaped in bolero outline above the waist. They are trimmed at their front edges with a row of gimp and a row of gimp along the edges of the revers forms a heading for a deep lace frill. At the lower ends of the revers a pretty arrangement of ribbon connects the side-fronts. The gown is closed at the center of the front over short basque-fronts of lining that are closed with hooks and eyes, or, when the gown is desired for a maternity gown, for which it is suitable, with lacing cords through metal eyes or worked eyelets. The back is in Princess-style and falls in flutes in the skirt. The sleeves are fancy at the wrists where they are trimmed with lace frills and are arranged to form short puffs at the top. A lace frill flares from the top of the standing collar over a ribbon stock.

Soft fabrics of all textures are appropriate for the gown and a single material used throughout or a color combination will be effective. Lace and ribbon will afford pretty trimming.

1897
Ladies' Costume

No. 8914 — The costume is here shown developed in white lawn over pink and yellow glacé taffeta. The seven-gored skirt is gathered at the back to hang in full folds and the flare at the bottom is in accordance with the latest demands of fashion. An attractive foot-trimming is afforded by a flounce of deep lace edging headed by a row of insertion on which bows of coral-pink ribbon are set over the seams at each side of the front.

The waist has a fitted lining and is closed in front. The fronts and back are gracefully full, the fullness being drawn becomingly to the center at the bottom by several rows of shirrings. The fullness in the front and back is framed by the tapering ends of frills that meet on the shoulders and then pass about the arms'-eyes, falling in ripples about the sleeves, which are in coat shape and are in this instance made in three-quarter length and finished with frills. Cross-rows of insertion decorate the full fronts and all the frills are trimmed at their edges with insertion and narrow lace. A frill of edging droops over a ribbon stock drawn about the standing collar and an effective disposal of ribbon on the sleeves and waist enhances the dressiness of the gown.

In the dainty development pictured, the gown will be copied by the fair residents of warm latitudes for day wear and by those living in colder climates for evening functions at which *décolleté* bodices are not imperative. Thin silks and tissues over silk are perfectly adapted to the mode and pearl trimmings with lace and ribbon will afford charming adornment.

1897 Ladies' Calling Costume

No. 9444. — The calling costume is an important matter at this season and a most excellent style is here pictured made of fine quality brown serge and velvet with braid, velvet and bands of Astrakhan combined in an elaborate decoration. The handsomely adorned basque is fitted with the greatest precision and closed diagonally from the right shoulder; a draped revers of velvet lined with silk is turned over from the closing with dressy effect. The basque is lengthened by a circular velvet peplum that is smooth at the front and sides and softly rippled at the back. The two-seam sleeves cling close to the arm to well above the elbow and are gathered at the top where they stand out stylishly; at the wrists they are completed with Astrakhan-trimmed ornaments that flare over the hand. A standing collar that is closed at the side and a softly wrinkled belt of velvet with frill-finished ends closed at the back are stylish completions.

The fashionable fan back distinguishes the five-gored skirt, which presents a moderate flare at the bottom and soft ripples at the sides.

The most conspicuously appropriate fabrics for this mode are broadcloth, which may be handsomely braided in scroll design, cheviot, that may be braided and fur trimmed, and the lovely zibeline and camel's hair weaves that come in the warm, rich shades appropriate for the season.

The hat has a soft crown of silk and ribbon and ostrich plumes trim it artistically.

1897 Misses' Party Dress

No. 8963 — The present development of this simple dress is charming, although inexpensive. Pink batiste was used for the making and the decoration of ribbon and Italian lace insertion and edging is exceedingly dainty. A full gathered skirt flows in free folds from the waist, which has a square yoke above a full front and full backs. The waist is closed at the back and is finished with a standing collar but a square neck may be arranged, if desired. Triple caps pointed at the center fall over puffs at the top of the close coat-sleeves.

The dress will be quite as pretty for afternoon wear in the summer as for party wear during the season immediately preceding. Soft silks and woolens, as well as the whole list of washable fabrics will make up with good effect by the mode.

Girls from ten to sixteen years of age wear this costume attractively.

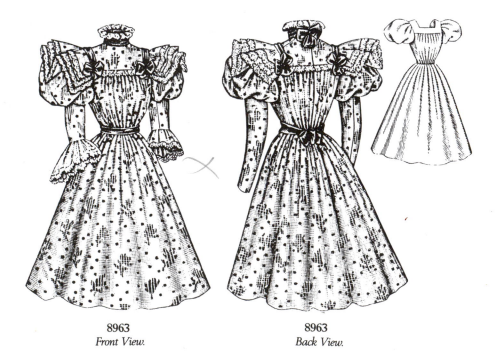

8963
Front View.

8963
Back View.

1897 Misses' Costume

No. 8955 — This is a most graceful and becoming style of costume for party, graduation or general wear, as it may be varied to suit different occasions, the pattern providing for a high, round or square neck and full-length, elbow or short puff sleeves. White organdy over blue silk was here selected for the costume and *mousseline de soie* and ribbon bows decorate it effectively. The waist has a lining fitted by single bust darts and underarm and side-back gores and the closing is made at the center of the back. The full front and full backs, which are joined in shoulder seams and separated by underarm gores, are gathered at the top and at the waist, the fullness being drawn well to the center; their upper edges, which may be square or rounding, are covered with a soft gathered ruche of *mousseline de soie*. In the high-necked waist, the lining is faced to give the effect of a yoke and a high standing collar is added. A ribbon bow gives a dainty decorative touch on each shoulder. A short, mushroom puff droops over the top of the two-seam sleeve which fits the arm closely. The sleeve may end at the bottom of the puff or may extend to the elbow or to the wrist, as preferred. The elbow sleeves are finished with a frill of *mousseline de soie* headed by ribbon prettily bowed at the outside of the arm. A wrinkled belt of ribbon surrounds the waist and is tastefully bowed over the closing.

The straight full skirt measures three yards and a half and the gored skirt three yards round at the bottom in the middle sizes. The full skirt is deeply hemmed at the bottom and gathered at the top all round; below the upper edge, across the front and sides, are four curved rows of shirring that produce a novel and pretty effect. The gored skirt is gathered at the back and smooth in front and at the sides. The skirts are completed together with a belt and the plackets are finished at the center of the back. Either skirt may be used alone, if desired.

For dressy occasions silk, organdy, dotted swiss, mull and *mousseline de soie* will be selected and if white is chosen, a becoming color of silk is used underneath. Ribbon, lace edging and ruffles or frills of *mousseline de soie* are available for decoration.

Pattern No. 8955 is for misses from twelve to sixteen years old.

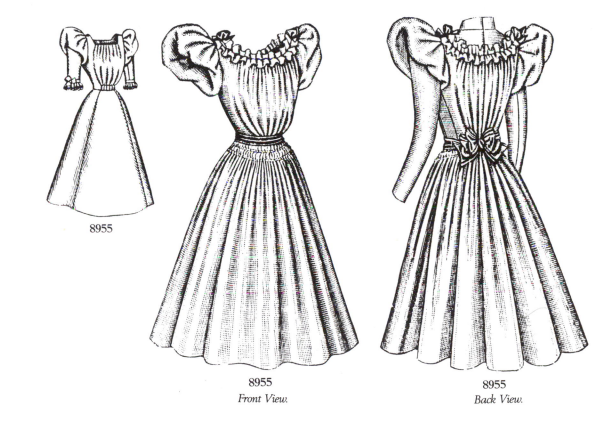

8955

8955
Front View.

8955
Back View.

1897 Misses' Russian Wrapper

No. 9446 — This charming wrapper is in Russian style and is pictured made of cashmere and decorated with fancy braid, lace edging and ribbon. The lining extends to basque depth and is fitted by single bust darts, underarm and side-back gores and a center seam and closed at the center of the front. The smooth sides are due to underarm gores and the full, seamless back is gathered at the upper part of the shoulder edges, the fullness being drawn to the center at the waist by shirrings. The front shows pretty fullness at the center collected in gathers at the neck and waist and drooping in pouch effect; it is slashed at the left side from the shoulder to a desirable depth so as to effect the closing in correct Russian style. A frill of lace edging follows the closing. Ribbon tie-strings are formed in two loops where they are tacked to the ends of the shirrings in the back and bowed at the center of the front. The full sleeves are arranged over two-seam linings; they are gathered at the top and bottom and finished with braid-trimmed wristbands to which a graduated frill of lace edging is sewed. The braid-decorated standing collar is closed at the left side.

The mode is adaptable to cashmere, Henrietta, inexpensive silk, vailing and the soft wool novelty weaves of delicate colors that are effective when adorned with a trifling amount of lace edging, ribbon and fancy braid.

It can be worn by misses from twelve to sixteen years old.

1897 Girls' Dress

No. 8925 — The dress is quite suitable for best wear as here represented in a combination of plaid wool goods and plain velvet in a harmonious shade. A square yoke appears above full backs that are gathered at the top and bottom, and the waist is closed at the back. Pretty fullness in the front puffs out stylishly, and upon the front are fanciful boleros that are decorated with frills of ribbon matching the ground color of the plaid. A ribbon frill rises from the top of the velvet standing collar and a similar frill edges the velvet roll-up cuffs. Butterfly puffs on the sleeves are drawn up at the center under ribbons that are arranged in bows on the shoulders. A straight full skirt hangs from the waist, the joining being concealed by a narrow velvet belt.

Neat and serviceable dresses can be made in this way of plain and plaid or checked woolens, with simple braid outlinings or novelty goods could be associated with a trifling amount of silk. A tasteful school dress was made of a blue plaid woolen, the boleros being of blue bouché cloth.

Five to twelve-year-old girls look most attractive in this garment.

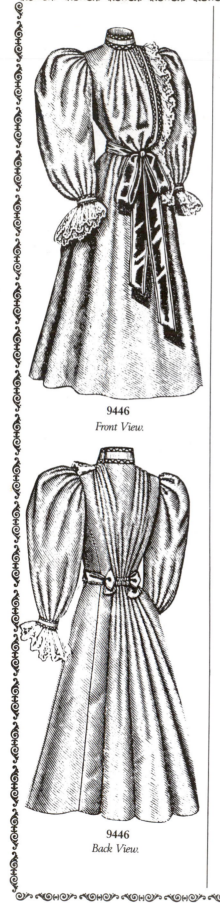

9446
Front View.

9446
Back View.

8925
Front View.

8925
Back View.

8925

1897 Girls' Dress

No. 8942 — This pretty little dress, which has the novel effect of a waist at the back and a loose front, is shown made of zibeline and trimmed with lace net, ribbon and lace edging. The dress has a body lining fitted by single bust darts and underarm and side-back gores and is closed invisibly at the back. The full waist backs extend to within square-yoke depth of the top on the lining and are gathered at the bottom and turned under and gathered at the top to form a frill finish. A full skirt, which is gathered at the upper edge, joins the lower edge of the body at the back, but at the front it is extended to lap over the body lining to within square-yoke depth of the top, its upper edge being turned in and gathered to form a frill finish, the side edges passing into the underarm seams. The upper part of the body lining is faced with the material overlaid with lace net to have the effect of a square yoke. On the coat-shaped sleeves at the top are arranged Empire puffs, over which droop deep fancy caps that are overlaid with lace net and shaped to form a point between two tabs. The edges of the caps are followed with frill of lace edging and the wrists are trimmed with a band of lace net and a frill of lace edging, the edging being contin- ued up the back of the wrist for a short dis-

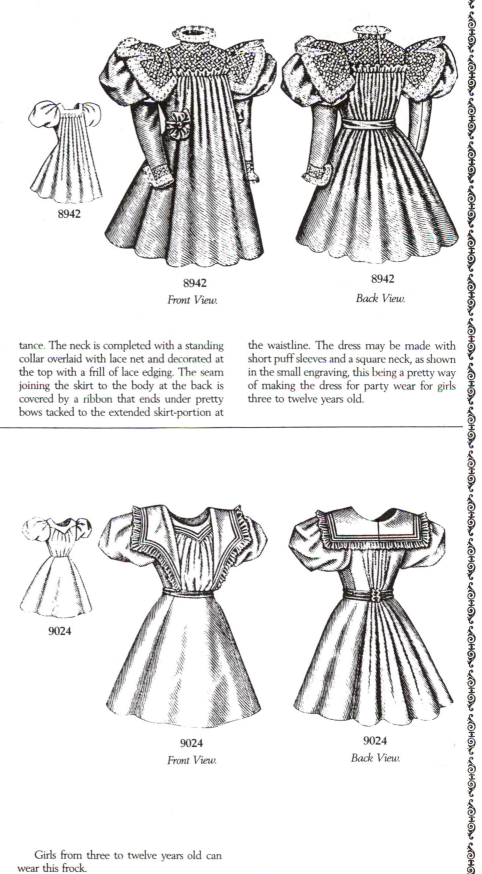

8942

8942
Front View.

8942
Back View.

tance. The neck is completed with a standing collar overlaid with lace net and decorated at the top with a frill of lace edging. The seam joining the skirt to the body at the back is covered by a ribbon that ends under pretty bows tacked to the extended skirt-portion at

the waistline. The dress may be made with short puff sleeves and a square neck, as shown in the small engraving, this being a pretty way of making the dress for party wear for girls three to twelve years old.

1897 Girls' Dress

No. 9024 — The dress is here illustrated made of soft woolen dress goods with a crush belt of silk and is trimmed with narrow velvet ribbon and plaitings of silk. The waist is made over a lining fitted by single bust darts and the customary seams; the closing is made at the back with hooks and eyes. Underarm gores separate the full front and full backs which are gathered at the top and bottom, the fullness being drawn well to the center at the back and drooping in blouse fashion in front. The neck is in low, round outline and a pointed yoke falls over the top of the full front. An effective feature of the dress is a fancy collar which falls deep and square at the back and extends down the front at each side of the fullness with the effect or large, fancy revers. Joined to the bot- tom of the waist is a four-gored skirt that is gathered at the back and smooth-fitting across the top at the front and sides, but ripples slightly below the hips. A crush belt with frilled ends encircles the waist and closes at the back. The short puff sleeve is gathered at the top and bottom and arranged over a one-seam lining.

The dress may be worn with or without a guimpe and may be made of China silk, crépon, cashmere, Henrietta, novelty goods, etc., with lace, velvet or satin ribbon, silk braid or gimp for a trimming.

9024

9024
Front View.

9024
Back View.

Girls from three to twelve years old can wear this frock.

1897 Childs' Dress

No. 8962 — This charming little dress is shown made of gray linen and trimmed with embroidered edging and cotton braid. The skirt is deeply hemmed at the bottom and in front it is extended to lap over a plain waist-front of lining to the neck, where it is gathered to produce pretty fullness between the boleros. The extended part passes into the shoulder and underarm seams and back of the underarm seams the skirt is gathered and joined to the lower edge of short waist-backs, which close at the center with buttonholes and buttons. The boleros round gracefully and their edges are decorated with a frill of embroidered edging and three rows of braid. The full sleeves are finished with wristbands that are trimmed to correspond with the narrow neckband. Three rows of braid decorate the skirt above the hem.

The simplicity and good style of the dress commend it for a great variety of washable fabrics. It is especially suitable for challis, inexpensive dimity, silk, lawn, organdy, nainsook and the durable linen and batiste fabrics now so highly favored. Ribbon, lace edging and braid are among the appropriate garnitures.

Children, ages one to six, can wear this dress.

8962
Front View.

8962
Back View.

8962

1897 Childs' Yoke Dress

No. 8956 — A very attractive little dress is here depicted made of nainsook and fancy tucking and trimmed with embroidered edging and featherstitching. The upper part of the dress is a square yoke that is fitted by shoulder seams and closed at the back with buttons and buttonholes. To the lower edge of the yoke is joined the full skirt which is gathered at the top and deeply hemmed at the bottom. The pretty square yoke-collar is made of fancy tucking and bordered with a frill of embroidered edging; it covers the yoke. A narrow featherstitched band and an upright frill of embroidery complete the neck. The full sleeves are gathered at the top and bottom and finished with wristbands of the tucking edged with a frill of embroidery.

Dainty little dresses may be fashioned according to this mode from organdy, lawn, fine cambric, nainsook and dimity, with trimming of lace or embroidered insertion and edging, hemstitching, ribbon-run beading, etc.

This pattern is for children six months to six years of age.

8956
Front View.

8956
Back View.

8956

1897 Little Girls' Costume

No. 9461 — Buff chambray is shown in the dress here illustrated. The plain body is fitted by shoulder and underarm seams and closed at the back. The skirt is gathered at the top across the sides and joined to the lower edge of the body, but is extended to lap over the body to the neck and shoulders at the front and back and is gathered at the neck. The neck is completed with a standing collar. The sleeves may be full length coat sleeves with short puffs at the top or they may be short puffs, as preferred. Neat frill caps are a becoming feature of the dress and fluff out prettily over the sleeves; they lower edges are followed by a frill of embroidered edging and a row of insertion. The collar and wrists are decorated to correspond.

Dimity, China silk, challis, cashmere and other seasonable materials suitable for children's dresses will be appropriate for developing this style and lace, embroidery and ribbon will provide a satisfactory decoration. Lace insertion may trim the skirt of an old rose cashmere gown.

Children ages one to six can wear this frock.

9461

9461

9461
Front View.

9461
Back View.

1511

9358

9263

1582

9259

1503

1575

9327

New Styles in House Garments 1898

1513

1514

9421

1504

1509

1507

9499

1512

1574

9239

1508

1898
Ladies' Costume

No. 1710 — A charming organdy costume in one of the new fluffy styles is here pictured, the fluffy effect, however, being produced entirely by the decoration. The waist, which is supported by a well-fitted lining, is closed at the center of the front and gathers at the neck and shoulder edges and closely lapped plaits at the waist, both back and front, adjust the fullness in soft pretty folds. Underarm gores give a close effect at the sides; the neck is finished with a standing collar, about which is arranged a ribbon stock having frill-finished ends closed at the left side. Double frill-caps fluff out in a most becoming way over the two-seam sleeves which are gathered at the top and have their fullness arranged in double puff effect by tackings to their coat-shaped linings. Lace-edged frills at the wrist and three rows of insertion bordered at each side with a frill of narrow lace trim the sleeves. A row of lace-edged insertion trims the waist from the shoulders down at the front and back, and another row covers the closing, giving quite an elaborate effect to a very simple waist. A wrinkled ribbon belt is finished with a stylish bow at the back.

The skirt is composed of seven gores and fits smoothly at the front and over the hips. It is gathered at the back, where it falls in soft folds and a bustle or any style of skirt extender may be worn, if desired. Four lace-edged ruffles of the material form quite an elaborate decoration; the lowest ruffle is put on straight around. The other three are arranged in zigzag effect and all the ruffles are finished to form self-headings.

Surah, taffeta and China and India silk, barège, nun's-vailing, plain or dotted Swiss, plain or embroidered nainsook, dimity and lawn are some of the materials suitable for a costume of this style. Lace or nainsook insertion and edging, satin or velvet ribbon will supply the garniture.

1710

1710
Front View.

1710
Back View.

74

1898 Ladies' Visiting Toilette

No. 9782 — Novelty dress goods and silk are combined in this toilette and silk and bands of insertion provide the decoration. The basque is especially commended for stout ladies, being fitted with two underarm gores at each side. The fronts open over a full vest of silk that is effectively framed by oddly shaped large revers which turn over from the front edges of the fronts. The fashionably shaped two-seam sleeves are gathered at the top and the close-fitting standing collar is becomingly trimmed with insertion.

A stylish feature of the five-gored skirt is the circular Spanish flounce, which is tastefully trimmed to accord with the basque. The skirt presents the admired smooth effect at the top in front and over the hips, and the back may be plaited or gathered. Trimmed skirts are multiplying in number and the Spanish flounce is conspicuous on many of the new modes, though not to the exclusion of band trimming, insertion, etc. This toilette will be excellent to copy in challis, lawn, organdy, grenadine and a long list of sheer fabrics now being made up. Fancy bands will be found in limitless variety to trim wool goods, and lighter textures will be beautiful by lace and ribbon. Chiffon or Liberty silk could be used for the vest.

1898 Ladies' Spring Costume

No. 9750 — The color blending in this toilette, tan grenadine and green silk, is very effective, and braid in plain and fanciful disposed unites with a stylish Scotch plaid ribbon stock-tie and a fancy leather belt in giving an admirable decorative completion. The Russian basque has novel features in the Bonheur collar and odd-looking Russian fronts and is rendered trim in adjusment by a fitted lining which is faced with the silk above the low-cut fronts to have the effect of a vest or chemisette. The fronts are lapped and closed in Russian style to the left of the center and droop slightly in the fashionable manner. A peplum is a stylish accessory and its rounding ends are apart at the front. The Bonheur collar has a rounding outline at the back and its wide ends terminate above the bust. The shapely two-seam sleeve has gathered fullness at the top and the inside seam is left open for a short distance at the wrist.

The five-gored skirt shows the newest lines and may be plaited or gathered at the back. It is most effectively trimmed.

Among the smartest styles is the Russian basque and nearly every shade of cloth and the hardy Scotch weaves of cheviot and heather mixture are represented in its development. It may be made to contrast with or match the skirt, as shown in the present instance, and velvet or braid may be used as a decorative finish.

The hat is trimmed with flowers, leaves and ribbon.

1898 Misses' Costume

No. 9641 — This novel and stylish costume is pictured made of camel's hair and silk and trimmed with silk plaiting, velvet ribbon in two widths and satin ribbon bows, belt and stock. The waist may be made with a high or low neck and with full-length or elbow sleeves and is made over a well-fitted lining closed at the center of the front. The back joins the fronts in shoulder and underarm seams and the blouse is gathered all the way round at the waist and tacked to the lining to produce the fashionable blouse droop. The left front is narrow and the right front, which is gathered at the top, is wide to permit the closing to be made at the left side in Russian style. A stylish effect is given by four deep tucks which pass about the figure under the arms, each tuck being headed by a row of narrow velvet ribbon. A yoke of silk evenly tucked is very attractive in the high neck, which is finished with a standing collar, a ribbon stock and a silk plaiting. A handsome square Bertha follows the square neck of the blouse; short puffs are arranged at the top of the two-seam sleeves which are completed at the wrist with a plaiting of silk.

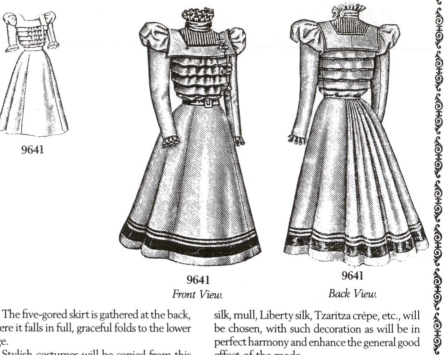

9641

9641
Front View.

9641
Back View.

The five-gored skirt is gathered at the back, where it falls in full, graceful folds to the lower edge.

Stylish costumes will be copied from this in cashmere, camel's hair, etc., and for evening and party wear, the lovely sheer organdies, inexpensive taffetas and gauzy fabrics such as silk, mull, Liberty silk, Tzaritza crépe, etc., will be chosen, with such decoration as will be in perfect harmony and enhance the general good effect of the mode.

Patern No. 9641 is suitable for young ladies from ten to sixteen years old.

1898 Misses' Promenade Costume

No. 1948 — The combination of cloth, tucked silk and velvet here seen in the costume is novel and particularly effective. The waist, which is cut in low, rounding outline to show a tucked silk yoke that is extended to the waist in front, is made with the fronts apart all the way and with becoming fullness that puffs out stylishly in front. Tab-shaped velvet Bertha portions edged with frills of silk gracefully finish the upper edges of the waist and extend round to the back where an invisible closing is made. The two-seam sleeves have their fullness arranged in short puff effect above a velvet fold arranged in an odd, pretty way, the decoration being repeated at the wrist.

The five-gored skirt is gathered at the back and has a pretty rippled effect at the sides. Charming decoration is given by a velvet fold that is arranged in a stylishly fanciful design. A crush silk belt is fastened at the left side under a bow.

Various other pretty combinations may be effected in the costume, and in the arrangement of decoration individual fancy may be gratified.

This is a suitable costume for girls ten to sixteen years old.

1948

1948
Front View.

1948
Back View.

1898 Girls' Costume

No. 2042 — Blue cashmere and plaid velvet were here employed in developing this exceedingly pretty dress, the beauty of which is much enhanced by the decoration of narrow velvet ribbon. The waist is made with a center-front and center-backs which are extended at the top to form a deep yoke that is shaped by shoulder seams. Full lower portions, joined in underarm seams, separate with a pretty flare over the center-front and center-backs; they are curved low at the top to shape a deep point where they lap on the center portions. The fullness at the bottom of the waist is collected in gathers and puffs out becomingly at the front, while at the back it is drawn down tight. The closing is made at the center of the back with buttons and buttonholes. A fitted lining imparts trimness to the waist which is finished with a standing collar. The two-seam sleeves which are made over coat-shaped linings have pretty fullness gathered at the top; on them rest smooth, oblong caps which shape a point at the front and back. To the bottom of the waist is joined the pretty four-gored skirt which is smooth at the top across the front, falls in rolling flutes below the hips and is gathered at the back.

The elaborate or simple development of the mode depends upon the material and garniture selected. All sorts of silk and wool materials are appropriate and ribbon, braid and lace will provide suitable decoration. A charming little frock is made of pink China silk, white applique lace covering the center-front and center-backs producing a very handsome effect. A row of the lace also trims the bretelles and skirt.

This attractive dress can be worn by five to twelve-year-old girls.

2042
Front View.

2042
Back View.

1898 Girls' Dress

No. 9635 — A charmingly simple little dress is here pictured made of gingham and decorated with embroidered edging. The fitted lining is closed at the back and supports the pretty low-necked blouse, which is gathered at the top and bottom and tacked to the lining to produce the stylish blouse droop. The dress may be made with a high or round neck, the lining being faced in round yoke effect in the high neck, which is finished with a standing collar. A fanciful Bertha bordered with embroidered edging and shaped to form points all round is sewed along the top of the blouse. Coat sleeves with short puffs at the top or short puff sleeves with a frill of embroidered edging at the bottom may be used, as illustrated. The straight full skirt is deeply hemmed at the bottom and gathered at the top and joined to the waist.

Bright shades of washable fabrics like gingham, chambray, etc., and also these materials in plaids, checks or stripes will be chosen for the dress.

Five to twelve-year-old girls will look attractive in this costume.

9635

9635

9635
Front View.

9635
Back View.

1898 Girl's Dress

No. 9823 — White lawn and fancy tucking are combined in the attractive dress here pictured front and backs are joined by underarm and shoulder seams and are gathered at the top and bottom, the front pouching stylishly; they are joined to a round yoke which is fitted by shoulder seams and the closing is made invisibly at the back. The dress may be made with or without a fitted body lining and with a high neck and close coat sleeves, or with a low neck and without sleeves to wear with or without a guimpe. The high neck is finished with a standing collar and the sleeves are finished at the wrist with a frill of lace edging headed by a row of insertion. Double, lace-edged frill caps stand out jauntily about the sleeves or arms. Three small tucks near their lower edges are exceedingly decorative. An applied belt, smooth and moderately broad, is overlaid with insertion; it conceals the gathers at the waist, giving a neat finish. A Bertha ruffle trimmed with a row of lace edging headed by a group of three tucks made at the edge to match the frill caps stands out smartly, giving the broad effect so desirable; a stylish four-gored skirt, which is gathered at the back and is smooth fitting at the top across the front and sides, is joined to the waist. The skirt is trimmed at the edge with a self-headed ruffle trimmed with tucks and edging to match the caps and Bertha. The tucks are merely decorative.

Charming little dresses of this style may be constructed from silk, organdy, dimity, gingham, linen and chambray, with a trimming of lace, embroidery, ruches of Liberty silk or chiffon and ribbon.

This pattern is suitable for five to twelve year olds.

9823

9823
Front View.

9823
Back View.

1898 Girls' Dress

No. 1706 — The dress is a particularly pretty simple style. It is here shown made of white organdy and trimmed with ribbon and an abundance of lace insertion and edging. The waist has a lining closely fitted by shoulder and underarm seams and single bust darts. The full front and full backs are gathered at the top and bottom, the front puffing out prettily, while the back is drawn down tight with the fullness well to the closing which is made at the center. The close-fitting two-seam sleeves have slight gathered fullness at the top and are encircled by a frill cap, upon which rest two gathered frills that end a little in front and back of the shoulders, the three being of graduated depth and giving a stylish breadth to the shoulders. The waist is completed with a standing collar. Three cross-rows of insertion decorate the front of the waist prettily, their position being designated in the pattern by lines of perforations. The full round skirt is gathered at the top and hangs from the body in pretty folds.

Silk, dotted and plain Swiss, lawn, gingham, challis, Henrietta, cashmere and vailings of all kinds are suitable for this frock; lace or embroidered edging and insertion may be utilized for decoration with charming effect. Red and white checked silk and lace edging are combined in a pretty frock and a tasteful decoration is supplied by narrow red ribbon ruchings, rows of it being arranged around the skirts, on the front of the waist and on the sleeves.

Pattern No. 1706 was developed for girls five to twelve years of age.

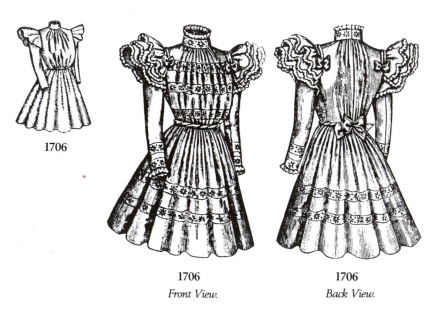

1706

1706
Front View.

1706
Back View.

1898 Childs' Dress

No. 1675 — White lawn and fancy tucking were here used for this pretty little dress. The dress portion, which has only very short shoulder seams, is gathered at the top across the front and back and is smooth at the sides; it is joined to a round yoke also shaped by shoulder seams and is finished at the bottom with a deep hem that is held in place by a row of fancy stitching. Gathered circular frills that stand out stylishly on the sleeves are included in the joining of the yoke and dress portion and are wide apart at the front and back; a narrow lace-edged frill follows the entire lower outline of the yoke, the whole creating a very dainty effect. The one-seam sleeves have pretty fullness collected in gathers at the top and bottom and are completed with wristbands trimmed with insertion and edging. The low standing collar corresponds with the wristbands. The closing of the dress is made at the back with buttons and buttonholes.

Nainsook, mull, percale, dimity, chambray, gingham, etc., are appropriate for the frock. A blue chambray dress may have the collar, wristbands and frills finished with white embroidered edging. When the dress is of silk the yoke may be of lace net and the trimming shirred baby ribbon.

This is an attractive pattern for children from six months to six years of age.

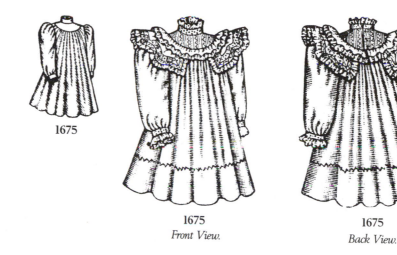

1675

1675
Front View.

1675
Back View.

1898 Childs' Costume

No. 1708 — Fine nainsook, embroidered edging and fancy tucking are here combined in this dainty little dress; narrow embroidered edging and insertion supply the decoration. The dress is made with a square yoke, shaped with shoulder seams and is gathered where it joins the lower edge of the yoke, the fullness falling in graceful folds to the lower edge which is finished with a deep hem. Only short shoulder seams fit the dress portion and all fullness is drawn away from the sides. The neck is finished with a narrow band of insertion which is trimmed at the top with a frill of edging. Included in the seams joining the dress portion to the side edges of the yoke are broad gathered frills of embroidered edging with mitred corners; they fluff out prettily on the one-seam sleeves which are gathered at the top and bottom and finished with wristbands trimmed to match the neckband. The closing is made at the back with buttons and buttonholes.

The dress may be made of light-weight woolen goods as well as the thinner fabrics, such as lawn, dimity, organdy, chambray, gingham, etc., and the hem may be hemstitched. Ruchings of ribbon or rows of insertion and embroidered edging may be applied in any desired manner to decorate these dresses.

This is a suitable costume for 6 month to six-year-old children.

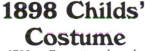

1708

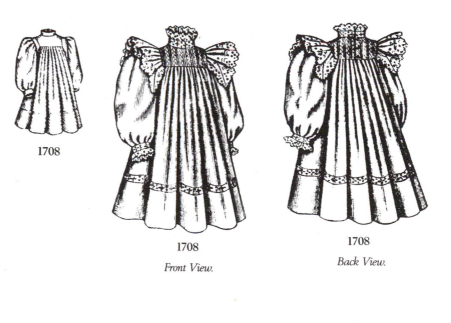

1708
Front View.

1708
Back View.

1899 Ladies' Costume

No. 2725 — Delightfully airy and summary in appearance is the charming gown here illustrated made of organdy. It is simply fashioned and tastefully trimmed with ribbon-edged ruffles of the material and a pretty disposal of narrow frilled ribbon. The waist, which is made over a fitted lining, has a pointed yoke of tucked organdy that fastens along the left shoulder. The standing collar, which also fastens at the left side, is made of the tucked organdy and a rippled flare portion gives a stylish finish to the collar. The fullness in the back and fronts of the waist is drawn well to the center at the top and at the waist by gathers, the fullness being caught down tightly at the back, while in front it is allowed to blouse stylishly. The closing of the fronts is made down the center with hooks and loops. The sleeves are fitted by inside and outside seams and are faced at the top in pointed cap effect with the tucked organdy. Narrow ruffles of the material edged with ribbon outline the yoke and the facings of the sleeves; narrow ribbon arranged in a scroll design gives an ornamental finish to the waist. The sleeves are completed with flare cuffs that fall gracefully over the hands.

The skirt is in seven-gored style and is smoothly fitted at the front and sides but has the slight fullness at the back underfolded in a box-plait. The original arrangement of the ribbon and ruffled decoration is very attractive.

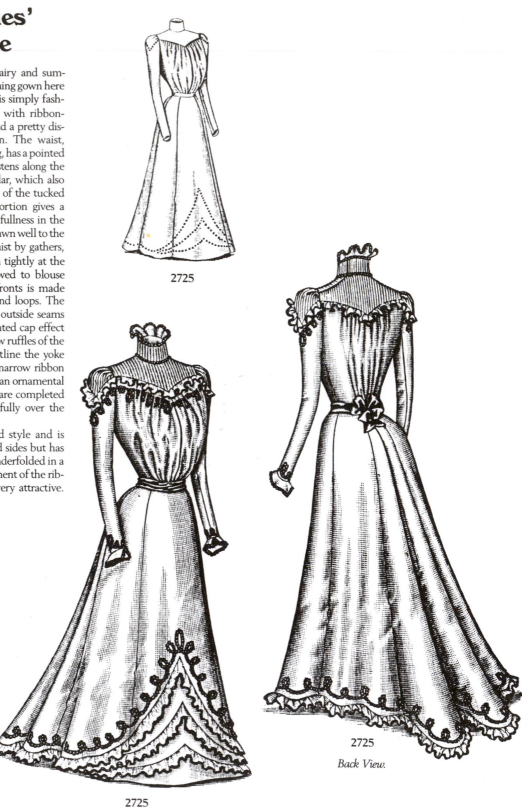

2725

2725
Front View.

2725
Back View.

1899 Misses' Costume

No. 3173 — A combination of materials is productive of very effective results in this stylish costume. Tan cashmere and white all-over lace over light blue silk are here associated. The waist shows the drop effect which is one of the season's most fashionable fancies. It extends to the line of the waist and is made with a dart-fitted lining on which are arranged the smooth center-backs and center-fronts that are extended to form a yoke and are joined in seams on the shoulders. The full side-portions separate in V outline at the front and back and have becoming fullness collected in shirrings at the bottom and gathered at the top to form a frill heading. The side-backs are straight across at the top, while the side-fronts are extended slightly upward toward the center; they blouse becomingly all around. The closing is made invisibly at the center of the back. The upper portion of the two-seam sleeve is hollowed out at the top to reveal a cap facing arranged on the smooth lining. It is finished with a gathered frill of the material that is in line with the frill heading formed on the side portions and emphasizes the drop effect. Oddly shaped cuffs that flare over the hands complete the sleeves.

The neck is finished with a standing collar having two fanciful turn-over portions that flare at the front and back.

The seven-gored skirt is perfectly smooth at the top all round. An underfolded box-plait is formed at the center of the back and falls in rolling folds to the lower edge. Bands of silk overlaid with lace and pointed at the bottom are arranged on all the seams of the skirt, except the center seam, with unique effect. The bands are of graduated lengths, being shortest at the back and extending below the knees at the front. A ribbon belt bowed at the back gives the final touch.

Cloth and any light-weight woolen material may be appropriately selected for the costume in combination with fancy tucking or plain silk, lace net, etc. Ribbon, braid or insertion will supply the garniture.

Patern No. 3173 is for misses from twelve to sixteen years of age.

3173
Front View.

3173
Back View.

1899 Misses' Costume

No. 3179 — A costume developed in fawn nun's-vailing combined with rose-colored satin that is revealed under an applique of all-over lace is here shown, applique lace edging and bias folds of the material supplying the trimming. The waist, which is made over a lining fitted by single bust darts and underarm and side-back gores, is fashioned with a plain round yoke that is seamed on the shoulders. The yoke is prettily revealed by the front and backs, which are separated by underarm gores and meet in short seams on the shoulders. At the top the backs and front are in fanciful low outline and at the waistline the slight fullness at the back is disposed in two backward-turning plaits at each side of the closing, while that at the front is gathered and allowed to droop becomingly. The waist is invisibly closed at the center of the back and on it is arranged a double bertha which is fancifully shaped to correspond with the graceful upper edge of the waist. The bertha is smooth and in two sections, the lower section being a little deeper than the upper one and the lower edges are slightly rounded. The neck is completed by a standing collar that is shaped to form flaring points at the back. The two-piece sleeve, which is made over a two-seam lining, is slightly gathered at the top and is finished by a circular cuff. A crush belt of rose-colored ribbon, which is closed with a fancy buckle at the front, encircles the waist. The collar may be made without the points, if preferred.

The skirt is made quite dressy by trimming folds and consists of five gores; it is fitted smoothly at the top and an under box-plait is formed at the center of the back, where the placket is made. Below the hips the skirt ripples symmetrically and at the back it falls gracefully in deep folds.

Blue serge may be combined with blue white shepherd's plaid for the costume, the plaid being used for the yoke and bertha. Nun'-vailing, barége, poplin, foulard, Venetian and any of the other popular silks would also prove satisfactory for the costume. A pretty and exceedingly dressy costume for a young miss could be of satin-striped challis, with the yoke and collar of tucked silk in a contrasting color and frills of satin ribbon for trimming.

Misses from twelve to sixteen years of age wear this costume attractively.

3179

3179
Back View.

3179
Front View.

1899 Girls' Dress

No. 3100 — The tendency in girls' frocks is toward simplicity of design. A charming example styled the Esther dress is here shown made of deep blue poplin, with white China silk for the guimpe, and tasteful ornamentation is contributed by applique lace and narrow ribbon. The dress is fashioned with a very short body, consisting of side-fronts and side-backs that are joined in underarm and shoulder seams and overlap a smooth center-front and center-backs. The body is in low, square outline and to it is joined the graceful full skirt which is gored at the sides where it is seamed. At the top the skirt is gathered and the body is closed with buttons and buttonholes at the back.

With the design is worn a guimpe that has full backs and a full front joined in underarm and shoulder seams and closed at the back with buttons and buttonholes. The guimpe is gathered at the neck all round and the fullness at the waistline is regulated by a tape inserted in a casing. A standing collar finishes the neck and the one-piece sleeve is gathered at the top and bottom, where it is finished by a wristband.

If colored piqué and all-over embroidery be used for the dress and white lawn for the guimpe, with piqué braid for decoration, a pleasing little frock will result.

Pattern No. 3100 is for girls from three to twelve years of age.

3100

3100
Front View.

3100
Back View.

1899 Girls' Costume

No. 3144 — At this time of year the mother's thoughts are, no doubt, busily occupied planning school dresses for the little maiden. A simple one is here shown developed in blue cashmere and trimmed with fancy braid. The waist, which is made over a plain lining fitted by single bust darts and underarm and shoulder seams, is originally designed. It has a full center-front topped by a smooth narrow yoke curved up prettily at the bottom and these portions are stylishly framed by the side-fronts, to which they are joined under side-plaits. The side-fronts are plain at the top, but have gathered fullness at the lower edge where, with the center-front, a slight pouch effect is given. A standing collar completes the neck and the dress closes at the back with buttons and buttonholes. The backs are slightly full at the bottom, and on the waist is arranged a scalloped cape-collar which is in two sections that meet at the back, while at the front they are included in the joining of the center-front and side-fronts for a short distance. The cape collar extends becomingly over the two-piece sleeve, which is gathered at the top, arranged over a lining and finished by a fancifully scalloped cuff that falls over the hand. The plain full skirt is gathered at the top and joined to the waist with a cording of the material.

Serge, cheviot, broadcloth, mohair or similar materials would also be appropriate for the mode and quillings of black satin ribbon may serve to give the decorative touch.

This dress is appropriate for girls from five to twelve years old.

3144

3144
Front View.

3144
Back View.

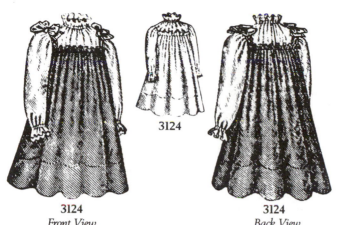

3124
Front View.

3124

3124
Back View.

Little Girls' Dress.

1899 Little Girls' Dress

No. 3124 — Rose-colored cashmere for the skirt and white surah silk for the yoke and sleeves are here combined in the simple dress, a guimpe effect being thus achieved. A dainty touch is given by shoulder ties of rose-colored ribbon. The dress is made with a full, seamless yoke which is applied on the plain body-lining. Shoulder and underarm seams adjust the body lining and the yoke is gathered at the lower edge and turned under and shirred at the neck to form a frill heading. The skirt laps over the body lining to the yoke and is plain at the sides, but in full gathered style both at the front and back, the upper edge being turned under and shirred to form a frill heading. The closing is invisibly effected at the center of the back, and the one-piece bishop sleeve, which is gathered at the top, is turned under and shirred a short distance from the lower edge to form a frill that falls over the hand.

Pattern No. 3124 is for little girls from one to six years of age.

1899 Little Girls' Costume

No. 3152 — Bands of heavy écru insertion relieve this otherwise plain dress, which is here shown made of pale-blue cashmere. The dress is fashioned with a plain square yoke seamed on the shoulder and has full lower portions joined in underarm seams and gathered at the top and bottom. The full portions are smooth under the arms and are arranged over a plain lining, which is adjusted by shoulder and underarm seams. The neck is finished by a narrow band, and the full one-piece sleeve, which is gathered both top and bottom, is completed with a narrow wristband. Smooth, scalloped caps stand out over the tops of the sleeves and the full gathered skirt is joined to the short body, which is invisibly closed at the back.

Little girls from one to six years of age will look attractive in this dress from pattern No. 3152.

3152
Front View.

3152

3152
Back View.

1899 Little Girls' Dress

No. 2518 — Blue cashmere was used for the attractive dress shown in the accompanying illustrations, and dark-blue ribbon supplies the garniture. The dress has a short body supporting the full skirt, which falls in folds all round. Smooth bretelles arranged over the shoulders extend to the lower edge of the body at the back and front and rest on gathered puffs arranged at the top of the two-seam sleeves. The standing collar is closed like the body at the back.

This is a suitable dress for one to six-year-old girls.

2518

2518
Front View.

2518
Back View.

1900 Ladies' Basque-Waist

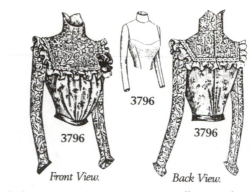

Front View. 3796 3796 *Back View.*

No. 3796 — The dainty waist is an exemplification of the charming possibilities of the guimpe modes. It is here pictured made of figured organdy and trimmed with a ruffle and ruching of the material and a ribbon bow, while all-over lace was chosen for the guimpe. The waist is fitted by underarm and short shoulder seams and arranged over a tight lining. The pouching front is noticeably full and is gathered at the top and bottom; the backs are plain save for scanty plaited fullness in the lower part at each side of the closing which is made at the center. The waist is sleeveless and is cut low and square at the neck; a crush ribbon belt gives the final touch.

With the waist is worn a separate guimpe that is adjusted by single bust darts and underarm gores and closed at the back. A fancy stock is at the neck and a flaring circular cuff is an attractive feature of the comfortable two-seam sleeve which is gathered at the top.

All-over embroidery, fancy tucking or revering may be used for the guimpe of a lawn or Swiss waist, while tucked satin or corded silk will be appropriate for the guimpe, if cashmere, silk or cloth be selected for the waist.

1900 Ladies' Skirt

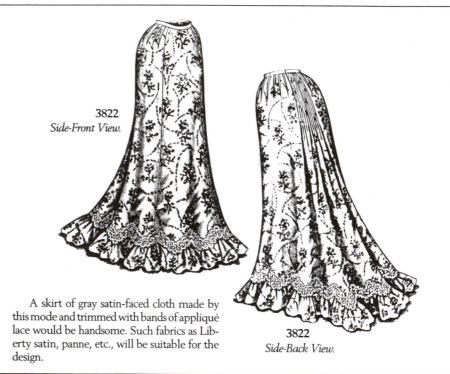

3822
Side-Front View.

3822
Side-Back View.

No. 3822 — Tucking seems to have gained a firm foothold in the world of fashion and appears quite as largely on skirts as on bodices this season. A very gracefully designed skirt is here shown developed in white India silk figured in light blue. The skirt has four gores — a front-gore, a wide gore at each side and a back-gore. The fullness at the back of the skirt is arranged in a box-plait on the outside, a group of backward-turning tucks appearing between the outer folds of the plait. The tucks are of even depth and extend about ten inches below the belt, the resulting fullness flaring gracefully to the lower edge. A cluster of tiny dart-shaped tucks that taper to points at the bottom removes the fullness over each hip and a ruffle of the material shaped in scalloped outline at the top and headed by a band of lace applique gives a pretty finish at the lower edge. The skirt, which may be made with a deep or in round length, is made over a five-gored foundation skirt that may be used or not and is fitted over the hips by a dart at each side.

A skirt of gray satin-faced cloth made by this mode and trimmed with bands of appliqué lace would be handsome. Such fabrics as Liberty satin, panne, etc., will be suitable for the design.

Seasonable Garments for Young Folks

1900 Girls' Sailor Costume

No. 3801 — Stylishness and comfort are the characteristics of this neat sailor costume which is represented made of blue serge and decorated with rows of white braid. The straight skirt is in full gathered style all around at the top and is supported by a plain body fitted by shoulder and underarm seams and closed at the back with buttons and buttonholes. A smooth shield is applied on the body which is finished by a shallow standing collar.

The blouse droops in the regulation way and is seamed on the shoulder and the sides; it is plain at the top, but has fullness at the bottom regulated by a tape or an elastic inserted in a hem. The fronts are closed in double-breasted fashion with buttons and buttonholes and above the closing are shaped to reveal the shield in V outline. On the blouse is arranged a stole sailor collar that is deep and square at the back and has broad ends that meet at the front. The collar, however, may have pointed ends, if preferred. Ribbon tie-ends prettily bowed just below the collar are tacked to the blouse on the inside and the one-piece sleeve, which is gathered at the top and bottom, is completed by a straight cuff.

3801

3801
Front View.

3801
Back View.

A costume of this type may be developed in cloth, flannel, piqué or duck and trimmed with braid.

Pattern No. 3801 is appropriate for little girls from two to eight years of age.

1900 Girls' Dress

No. 3829 — Pink lawn and fancy embroidered tucking are here united in the development of the dainty dress. Decoration is supplied by embroidered edging and insertion, the arrangement of the latter being exceedingly effective. The fronts and backs of the waist are shaped in low scalloped outline at the top where they are perfectly smooth. The front edges of the fronts overlap at the center, and the fronts puff out at the bottom where there is becoming fullness collected in shirrings. The backs overlap to correspond with the fronts and the fullness in the lower part is drawn down close by shirrings at each side of the invisible closing. The smooth yoke is shaped with shoulder and short underarm seams and closed at the back. A standing collar finishes the neck. The drop effect is carried out in the two-seam sleeves, which are cut away at the top on the upper side to reveal a cap-facing arranged on the two-seam lining. The three-piece skirt consists of a front gore and two circular portions that are seamed at the center of the back, and has becoming fullness regulated by gathers at the top all round. The skirt is joined to the waist, which is made over a dart-fitted lining and a ribbon belt is worn.

3829
Front View.

3829
Back View.

Vailing, cashmere, and other lightweight woolens, as well as washable cotton fabrics, may be used with pleasing results for the dress. Braid, ribbon or insertion and plaitings of silk will supply appropriate garniture. Cream-white challis showing a floral design in forget-me-nots will combine prettily with fine white lace tucking for the dress, with black velvet ribbon for a belt, stock and shoulder bows.

Pattern No. 3829 was developed for girls from five to twelve years of age.

1900 Little Girls' Costume

No. 3790 — The quaint little frock is characterized by a long waist. It is here pictured made of chambray and all-over embroidery and is decorated with embroidered edging and beading. Three box-plaits are taken up at the front and back of the waist, which is closed with buttons and buttonholes under the middle box-plait at the back. The waist is fitted by shoulder and underarm seams and is low and square at the neck, where it is finished by a fanciful smooth bertha, the ends of which meet at the back. The cap sleeve is circular and is narrowest under the arm where it is seamed. The straight skirt, which is in full gathered style all around, is attached to the waist, the joining being concealed by a wide sash artistically bowed at the back.

Gingham and tucking, organdy and all-over lace, white and blue piqué, brown and red linen, etc., may be chosen for the dress with satisfactory results.

Pattern No. 3790 was designed for little girls from two to eight years of age.

3751

3751
Front View.

3751
Back View.

1900 Girls' Dress

No. 3751 — A dainty frock for the wee tot is here shown made of sage-green cashmere and black silk with a trimming of cream lace edging. The dress is low and square at the neck, where the fullness in the front and back is collected at the center in rows of shirrings to form a frill heading. The dress is shaped by underarm and short shoulder seams and is made over a short body-lining that is faced to yoke depth with silk and topped by a standing collar. Fanciful bretelles stand out over the gathered tops of the two-seam sleeves which, however, may be replaced by the short puff sleeves gathered at the top and bottom and made over smooth linings. If a low-necked dress be desired, the body lining is cut out to correspond with the neck of the dress.

A pretty dress for party wear could be made of pale pink China silk with lace edging or chiffon ruches for decoration. The design is also suitable for reproduction in wash materials.

Little girls from two to eight years of age will look most attractive in this dress.

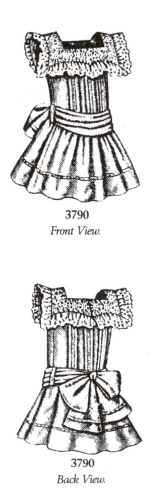

3790
Front View.

3790
Back View.

1900 Girls' Costume

No. 3809 — This serviceable and at the same time very pretty little frock for wear with a guimpe is represented made of striped gingham and insertion, decoration being supplied by ruffles of embroidery. The straight, full skirt is gathered at the top both at the front and back and is joined to a shallow square yoke smoothly fitted by shoulder seams. The yoke is entirely concealed by a smooth square bertha made of insertion. The corners of the bertha are mitred and the ends meet at the back where the closing of the dress is made with buttons and buttonholes. The bertha stands out over the short puff sleeves which are gathered at the top and bottom and completed by narrow bands.

The dress may be made of lawn or organdy combined with fancy tucking or lace insertion for the bertha and adorned with deep frills of lace. Guimpes of lawn, organdy, Swiss and similar fabrics may be appropriately worn with the dress. Wool and silk goods are also appropriate for developing the dress in combination with velvet for the bertha.

Pattern No. 3809 is for little girls from two to seven years of age.

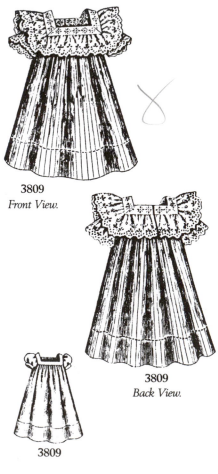

3809
Front View.

3809
Back View.

3809

1903
Misses' Costume

No. 6570 — Tan cloth was used in the construction of this dress, with bias bands of brown velvet dotted with French knots in black silk for decoration. Support is afforded by a fitted lining, the waist blousing slightly at the back and more pronouncedly in front. Two circular ruffles in bolero effect adorn the bodice and are overlapped by the yoke, which is shaped by shoulder seams and topped by a band collar. The closing at the back is invisibly made. Circular ruffles, in seeming continuation of those on the bodice, cap the sleeves which are of the bishop type. A soft ribbon belt is worn.

A circular flounce is applied to the three-piece foundation skirt, which has a habit back. The circular upper skirt is adjusted by darts and the fullness at the back is disposed in an inverted box-plait.

Olive-green albatross would be effective with narrow bands of Persian trimming outlining the edges. Henrietta, challis, veiling, étamine or silk give pleasing results.

This costume is appropriate for misses from thirteen to seventeen years old.

1903 Girls' or Misses' Blouse Dress

No. 6589 — A triple strap collar is the point of interest in this dress. Attractive developments are shown in red serge and pale blue nun's-veiling in combination with silk and fancy braid. A fitted body-lining supports the waist which is plain at the back and has a group of tucks in front stitched to yoke depth. The body blouses all around, and fashionable breadth is given the shoulders by the strap collar formed of three circular sections, the top one of which is extended to form tab ends. A standing band may be added to the neck and full or three-quarter length bishop sleeves are provided. The three-piece skirt is attached to the body and an inverted box-plait is arranged at the back where the fastening is made. A silk band bordered with fancy braid ornaments the lower edge and a ribbon sash is an attractive accessory.

White albatross with Persian silk and narrow Persian trimming would be in good taste.

Pattern 6589 can be worn by girls from five to fourteen years of age.

1903 Ladies' Tucked Empire House Dress

No. 6605 — Here is a charming exponent of the Empire modes in a union of pale lavender crêpe de chine, panne velvet of a deeper tone and all-over lace, elaborated with narrow velvet ribbon and juby trimming. A fitted lining provides a foundation for the short body which may be high-necked with a band collar or in Pompadour style, a fancy collar bordered by a frill of the material giving a finishing touch. The pattern also makes allowance for a Dutch square neck and the closing is arranged on the left shoulder and the left side of the front. Tucks take up the fullness of the gown where it is attached to the short body and are stitched to knee depth, below which it is allowed to fall in a medium sweep or dip round length. Four or fewer band-frills may ornament the lower edge, producing a becoming flare. The sleeves are furnished with two-seam linings and are tucked to elbow depth, puffing out stylishly in full length over deep cuffs, or they may be banded closely in three-quarter length.

Red cashmere with the fancy collar elaborately embroidered with black, and with accessories of black miroir velvet or taffeta, suggests pleasing possibilities, or pink crêpe albatross will respond gracefully to the requirements of the mode. Peau de soie, soft silks, Henrietta, challis and crêpe de Paris are also suitable.

6605

6545

6579

6600

1903 Ladies' Waists and Skirt

No. 6600 — Dark gray cheviot provided material for the practical skirt and machine-stitching supplied the finish. Seven gores were used to give it the correct shaping, an extra gore forming an outside box-plait at the back, which is one of fashion's recent revivals. The closing is effectively concealed by the plait and the pattern makes provision for short round, instep or shorter (or outing) length. A measurement of about three yards and three-fourths is allowed at the lower edge in the medium sizes.

A skirt that will render excellent service may be reproduced in dark blue cravenette or any of the rain-proof materials and will be appropriate for stormy weather and general outdoor wear. Heavy skirtings and double-faced goods, storm serge, melton, cheviot and tailor suitings are adaptable. The seams may be strapped or covered with narrow braid if desired, or plainly finished with stitching.

1903 Ladies' Tea-Gown

No. 6594 — A unique feature of the tea-gown of pale blue cashmere elaborated with applique is the Monte Carlo bolero front, although the gown is complete without it. The back fits snugly and the fronts, which may be supported by a lining, have underarm darts and are shaped with generous fullness. A broad sailor collar edged with lace affords a becoming finish for the open neck but if a high neck be desired, the lining may be faced with the material and a band collar added. The bolero fronts are plaited and meet at the center. A band of applique heads the circular flounce, which is a discretionary feature, and the skirt should be cut away beneath it. Bishop sleeves in full length or in long elbow style may give place to flowing sleeves lengthened by lace frills. The full fronts may be confined by ribbon ties with long loops and ends.

Pale green crêpe albatross ornamented with black velvet ribbon and French lace would please dainty tastes. For service, red Henrietta trimmed with black taffeta and fancy braid will be practical, as will lady's-cloth, prunella and Lansdowne.

1903 Ladies' Shirt-Waist Costume

No. 6591 — The indications are that the skirt-waist costume has come to stay and many pleasing designs are being introduced. One of the prettiest modes is depicted in albatross, plain and patterned all over with collar, vest and cuffs of heavy white lace. Further ornamentation is afforded in the embroidered turnovers on the collar and cuffs. The box-plaited waist is provided with a fitted lining and the fronts separate all the way to disclose the vest, which is secured under a plait at the left side. A narrow band completes the neck, and the collar describes a deep point in front. Box-plaits give style to the sleeves and furnish fullness for puffs drooping over deep cuffs.

The five-gored skirt is box-plaited to flounce depth and the back fullness is disposed in an inverted box-plait. A graceful flare marks the lower edge, where, in the medium sizes, a measurement of about four yards and three-fourths is allowed. A medium sweep or dip round length may be adopted.

Changeable taffeta would make a rich and stylish costume with accessories of Venetian all-over. Checked Louisine is also greatly favored. A satisfactory reproduction would be in wool poplin with the vest and collar of white lace. Nun's-veiling, brilliantine, piqué, cotton cheviot, madras and challis are recommended.

1903 Girls' or Misses' Costume

6583

No. 6583 — The blouse modes are always favorites and characterize many of the newest dresses. Cream white albatross furnishes a pleasing example, applique band and ribbon providing the decoration. A fitted body lining gives support. A pointed yoke of all-over lace tops the blouse body and is outlined by a slashed bertha complemented by a ribbon tie in front. Sleeves of bishop shaping and a band collar are used. Tucks stitched for a short distance are introduced in the circular skirt which is attached to the waist and has an inverted box-plait at the back. A ribbon is adjusted about the waist and jauntily bowed over the closing at the back.

Red serge trimmed with black fibre braid would be pretty and serviceable. Pale blue Louisine would unite effectively with tucked white mousseline and white galloon. Also, attractive developments could be made in cashmere, Henrietta, challis, veiling and Lansdowne.

Pattern No. 6583 was developed for girls and misses from five to fourteen years old.

1903 Girls' or Misses' Blouse Dress

No. 6589 — A triple strap collar is the point of interest in this dress. Attractive developments are shown in red serge and pale blue nun's-veiling in combination with silk and fancy braid. A fitted body lining supports the waist which is plain at the back and has a group of tucks in front stitched to yoke depth. The body blouses all around and fashionable breadth is given the shoulders by the strap collar formed of three circular sections, the top one of which is extended to form tab ends. A standing band may be added at the neck and full or three-quarter length bishop sleeves are provided. The three-piece skirt is attached to the body and an inverted box-plait is arranged at the back where the fastening is made. A silk band bordered with fancy braid ornaments the lower edge and a ribbon sash is an attractive accessory.

White albatross with Persian silk and narrow Persian trimming would be in good taste.

This dress can be worn by five to fourteen year olds.

6589

1903 Girls' Dress

No. 6553 — Simplicity characterizes the dress represented here in mixed suiting and also in dark blue serge. The square yoke is a feature of the mode which is topped by a standing collar. Gathers regulate the fullness of the waist, where it joins the yoke and also at the lower edge. A back closing is effected with buttons and a lining may give support. Regulation bishop sleeves, closely banded, are employed. Gathers dispose of the fullness at the back of the skirt which consists of four gores and is attached to the waist, a belt concealing the joining.

Checked or striped plaid materials are suitable for school wear. A dress of blue Henrietta and white silk would be pretty.

Pattern 6553 is suitable for girls from four to fourteen years old.

6603

1903 Girls' Costume

No. 6603 — A pleasing combination is displayed in this frock made of sage-green cashmere and peau de soie of a darker shade. A lining provides a foundation for the plaited body, which is characterized by a pointed yoke separating with the fronts to disclose a vest of the silk. A standing collar finishes the neck, and the waist, closing at the back, blouses all around. Caps in drop-shoulder effect top the bishop sleeves and cuffs afford completion. The skirt is of the five-gored type, kilt-plaited, and joined to the body under a crush belt of ribbon.

Wool lace over silk would make an effective decoration for a dress of brown hop-sacking. Equal success may be achieved by uniting silk or velvet with canvas, voile, Henrietta, peau de crêpe, checks, or plaids.

Children from five to fourteen years old will look attractive in this costume.

1903 Girls' French Dress

No. 6548 — White piqué was trimmed with edging, insertion and buttons in the dress represented here. The mode is in French style and displays a long waist that has fullness at the lower edge and at the top, where it is cut out to accommodate the yoke applied to the lining. Low, square outline may be given the neck if preferred, and unique bretelles extending over the shoulders add to the attractiveness of the mode. Full-length bishop sleeves are provided but may be replaced by pretty cap sleeves slashed on the outside. The attached skirt is of the four-gored type with the fullness at the back disposed in gathers. A ribbon is crushed about the waist, ending in a bow at the back. A standing collar is supplied for the high-necked development.

Pastel pink l'Aiglon silk would make a dainty dress if trimmed with Mechlin lace and crystal buttons. A white organdy frock would be pretty with Valenciennes lace. Henrietta, China silk, lawn, dimity and cotton cheviot are suitable.

Pattern No. 6548 was designed for girls from three to ten years of age.

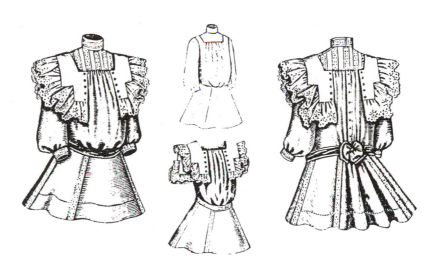

1903 Little Girls' Dress

No. 6557 — Thin white materials trimmed with lace or embroidery make the most satisfactory frocks for children. The dainty possibilities of nainsook are admirably set forth in the little dress and the square yoke of fancy tucking is a prominent feature. Provision is made for high neck with a band of ribbon-run beading or for Dutch round or square neck. A bertha of needlework may outline the yoke, giving breadth to the shoulders. A deep hem headed by hemstitching or insertion completes the lower edge. Sleeves of one-seam bishop shaping in full or elbow length, or in short puff style gathered into bands to correspond with the neck-band, may be chosen, frills of edging decorating them in the last two instances.

Little girls from six months to six years wear this dress attractively.

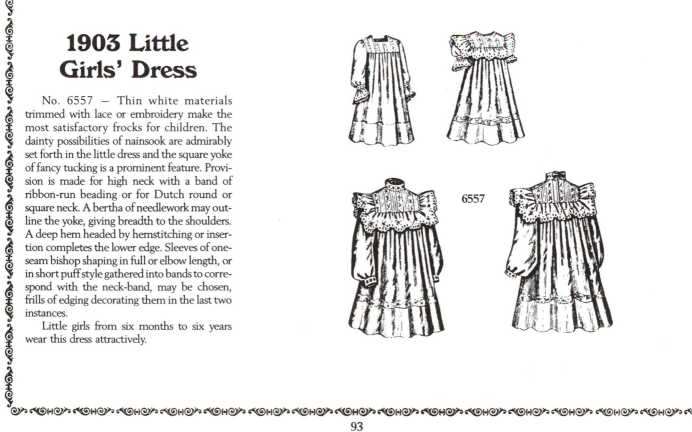

6557

1903
Childs' Dress

No. 6582 — The association of nainsook, fancy tucking, ribbon-run beading and edging is charming in the little frock depicted here. The round yoke, closing at the back, is of the fancy tucking topped by a shallow band with a bow of ribbon at the back but, if preferred, a Dutch round outline may be adopted. The full skirt is gathered to the yoke, where a double or single bertha forms a dainty finish and stands out broadly over the shoulders. Full-length or elbow sleeves of bishop shaping or short puff sleeves may be employed. The lower edge is turned under and hemstitched to position.

Fine white organdy would make a dainty dress and would combine advantageously with Mechlin lace insertion and edging. White is the choice for children's dresses and the fabrics especially recommended are linen and Victoria lawn, cambric, India linon, dimity, figured, striped and checked muslins, China or mignonne silk and the soft woolen materials.

Pattern 6582 can be worn by boys or girls from six months to six years of age.

1903 Girls' Dress

No. 6604 — Originality of design distinguishes the frock of dahlia-red albatross and applique band and black velvet ribbon produce pleasing contrast. A becoming feature is the triple bertha of circular shaping set on under a strap having long, pointed ends. The round yoke is applied to the lining, which may be used or not, as preferred. A standing collar completes the neck. Two box-plaits are introduced in the front of the waist, to which a pouching effect is given. A back closing is effected and slight gathers are used at the lower edge. Box-plaits appear at the top of the sleeves, the fullness below sagging over the wristbands. The circular skirt is attached to the waist and may have an inverted box-plait or gathers at the back. A strap-belt is a stylish accompaniment.

Marengo-brown basket cloth would unite charmingly with muguet lace and green velvet, or white Lansdowne would be pretty with perforated broadcloth over yellow satin.

This dress can be worn attractively by six to fourteen year olds.

1903
Misses' Dress

No. 6577 — A pointed bertha is the prominent feature of this dress. Royal blue velveteen, white taffeta and Russian applique were united to attain the result illustrated. The body of the dress is bloused modishly over the lining and may be topped by a tucked yoke and band collar or cut away for the low necked development. Bishop sleeves of the silk are overhung by cap sleeves which may be used alone if preferred. The attached skirt is of circular shaping and fits smoothly all around having an inverted box-plait or gathers at the back. A soft crush belt of Liberty satin ribbon ornaments the waist, ending in a rosette bow at the back where the closing is effected.

Lettuce green albatross would combine prettily with white l'Aiglon silk and French applique lace. Red and blue plaid with plain blue or red silk would make a serviceable frock and cashmere, cheviot, basket-cloth and canvas can be used.

Pattern No. 6577 was designed for five to fourteen-year-old misses.

1903 Girls' Frock

No. 6547 — Even when elaborately trimmed, white wash dresses have an air of simplicity that is eminently appropriate for children. No material is better adapted to these charming little frocks than fine India lawn. It was selected for making the dress illustrated with lace insertion, edging and ruffles of the material used for trimming. A round yoke formed of alternate rows of insertion and material tops the mode and a ruffle in bertha effect is added. A high or Dutch neck may be employed. The long full body, pouching slightly, joins the yoke under the ruffle. The full skirt is attached to the body and may be trimmed with insertion and elaborated by a lace-edged ruffle, or the latter may be dispensed with, a deep hem providing the finish. Bishop shaping characterizes the sleeves to which either full or elbow length may be given. The cuffs and the band finishing the high neck match the yoke. A sash is a pleasing accessory. The body lining may or may not be used.

Batiste is a frequent choice for little girls' dresses and would develop attractively from this pattern united with Mechlin lace.

Three to fourteen-year-old girls can wear this costume.

1903 Misses' Dress

No. 6583 — The blouse modes are always favorites and characterize many of the newest dresses. A fitted body-lining gives support. A pointed yoke of all-over lace tops the blouse body and is outlined by a slashed bertha complemented by a ribbon tie in front. Sleeves of bishop shaping and a band collar are used. Tucks, stitched for a short distance, are introduced in the circular skirt, which is attached to the waist and has an inverted box-plait at the back. A ribbon is adjusted about the waist and jauntily bowed over the closing at the back.

Red serge trimmed with black fibre braid would be pretty and serviceable. Pale blue Louisine would unite effectively with tucked white mousseline and white galloon and attractive developments could be made in cashmere, Henrietta, challis, veiling and Lansdowne.

Pattern No. 6583 can be worn by girls from five to fourteen years old.

1904 Ladies' Gown

1904 Girls' Costume
WOOLLAND BROTHE

Special House for

CHILDREN'S
CONFECTIONS,
For all ages
up to
16 years

No. 1 — Pretty dancing frock in soft silk trimmed with many insertions of fine lace. The bodice is enhanced with a dainty collar. Suitable for girls from six to ten years of age.

No. 2 — Delightful frock made of ring-spotted net over white silk. The bodice is embellished with silk motifs and the waist finished with a pink sash. Suitable for young ladies from six to twelve years of age.

No. 3 — Charming frock made of Valenciennes lace and embroidery over silk. Suitable for girls from one to three years of age.

No. 4 — Frock fashioned in ivory spotted Brussels net over silk; arranged with many frills of the same, outlined with soft silk and further adorned with lace and ribbon beading. Suitable for misses from seven to ten years of age.

No. 5 — Dressy frock in finest nainsook, tucked and profusely trimmed with real Valenciennes insertions and ribbon.

No. 9272

No. 9272   No. 9290

No. 9290

1905 Ladies' Gown

Nos. 9272-9290 — Crêpe de chine in one of the new shades of blue was chosen to make this charming gown, but any other silk or woolen that is not too heavy can be suitably employed, or if made with a low neck for balls, fashionable dinners, etc., any fashionable evening fabric can be used. Our model has a full front of the crêpe de chine gathered with a heading onto a square yoke of all-over lace in a stylish ecru shade laid over silk of the same tint. The back where the closing is formed is finished in the same manner. Straps of the lace bound with the crêpe de chine run over each shoulder. The sleeves are very novel and pretty and have short puffs adorned for half their length with shirred tucks and shirred into the long fitted cuffs of the material, trimmed iwth a band of lace bound like the straps. A deep shirred girdle of the material completes the bodice at the waistline but this can be omitted, if desired.

The skirt is cut with five gores and lengthened by a shirred flounce. It is trimmed with a band of all-over lace bound with silk to correspond with the waist garnitures.

1905 Ladies' Blouse Waist

No. 8381 — The mode here pictured in figured crêpe de chine and silk batiste is of the popular blouse order and closes at the back, the fullness being either drawn down or bloused, as preferred. A double box-plait marks the centre of the front. The lace yoke is in fancy outline and is designed for a high neck with standing collar or for Dutch round outline. A girdle is crushed about the waist and fastens at the back. The sleeves are wrinkled in mousquetaire style over close linings and in full or three-quarter length. A tight-fitting body lining is also supplied.

A yoke of embroidered white chiffon over silk will be exceedingly pretty for a waist of champagne crêpe Leda.

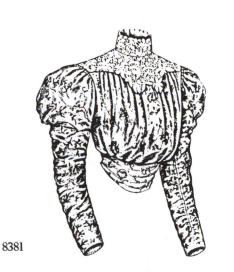

8381

1905 Ladies' Shirt Waist

No. 8380 — A pretty skirt waist of the lingerie order is here pictured in fine India linon, with adornment of lace, and in sheer batiste. Fine tucks to yoke depth at the back and front add to the good effect and the resulting fullness below is drawn down or eased. A yoke in clover design is an up-to-date feature, a neckband and standing collar affording neck completion. An invisible back closing is arranged. Deep cuffs or shallower ones are used to finish the sleeves. A soft belt of ribbon is used.

Nainsook, lawn, handkerchief linen, mousseline, crêpe de chine and China silk are among the best selections.

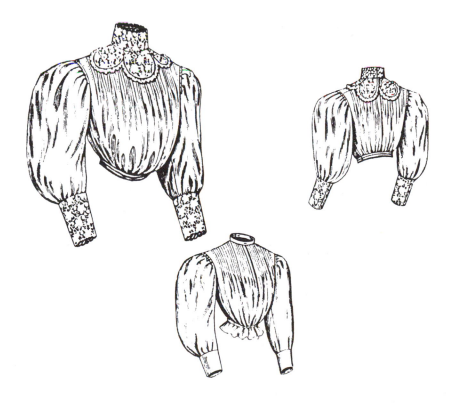

Medium Sweep.

Round Length.

1905 Ladies' Seven-Gored Skirt

No. 8375 — The flounce skirts are popular again, their graceful outline and general becomingness accounting for this fact. Dark blue broadcloth and mixed suitings are displayed in the illustrations, with machine-stitching for a finish. The mode, which is equally stylish without the flounce, is shaped by seven gores, rippling smartly below the hips where it shows a close adjustment. An inverted box-plait takes up the fullness at the back and a long or medium sweep as well as round length is allowed. When the flounce is used, the gores need not extend beneath it but this, however, is a matter of preference.

A smart walking costume might be made of bronze-green cloth with a skirt of this description and a long coat, tailor-finished. Tweed, etamine, serge, cheviot, voile, mohair, linen, piqué, duck and many of the heavy wash fabrics are durable materials for the mode.

Long Sweep.

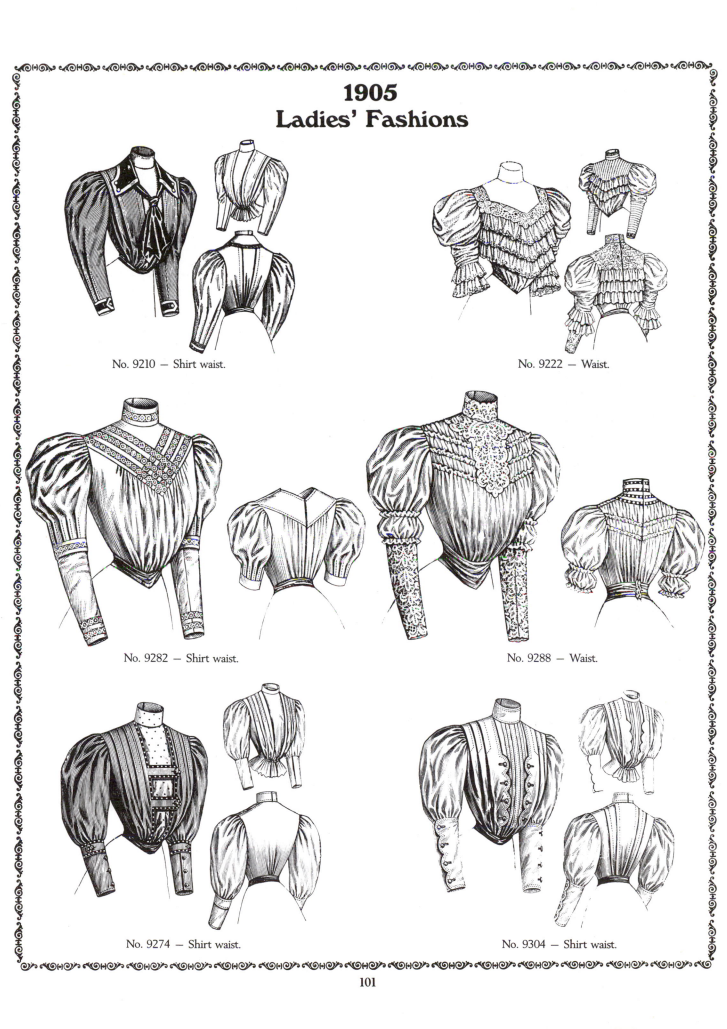

No. 9210 — Shirt waist.

No. 9222 — Waist.

No. 9282 — Shirt waist.

No. 9288 — Waist.

No. 9274 — Shirt waist.

No. 9304 — Shirt waist.

1905
Ladies' Fashions

No. 9288 — This charming design is suited to silks, light woolens, net, lace, and so on. Our model is of blue chiffon taffeta, made with a yoke of a lighter shade of velvet. This yoke is trimmed with fancy white silk braid and is cut in a deep pointed tab in the front and is short and rounded in the back. The front fullness is gathered into the shoulder seams and is shirred across on each side of the tab point of the yoke in three rather deep, shirred tucks, the lowest at deep yoke depth. The waist closes in the center back and is gathered on the shoulders and beneath the yoke in the same manner as the front and has two shirred tucks running across it.

No. 9300 — This dainty winter shirt waist is made of dark brown chiffon taffeta with a yoke of heavy tan colored linen embroidered in light blue and edged with fancy brown and tan silk braid. The front is tucked in box-pleat effect straight down the center and has groups of tiny tucks to yoke depth on each side of this. The closing is made in the center back with buttons and buttonholes, and the waist fullness is tucked for a short distance beneath the yoke on either side of the closing. The sleeves are full at the shoulders and are gathered just below the elbows into fitted cuffs of the material headed and edged with the fancy braid.

This waist is very dressy if made up of white taffeta or crêpe de chine with a yoke of allover lace.

No. 9300 — Ladies' shirt waist

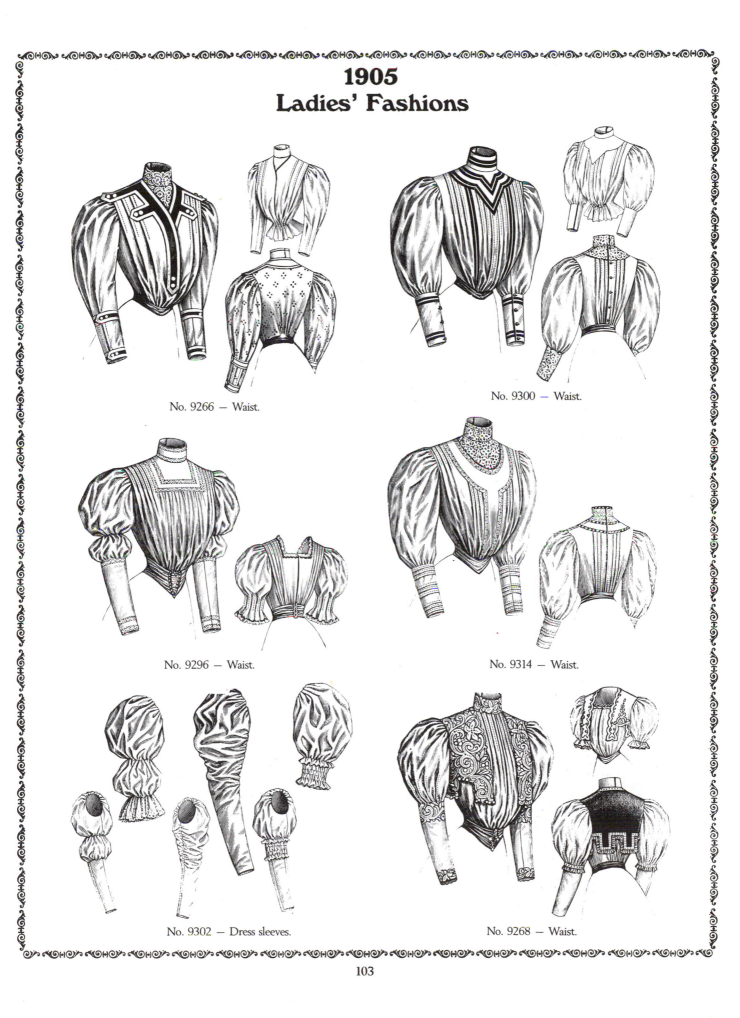

No. 9266 — Waist.

No. 9300 — Waist.

No. 9296 — Waist.

No. 9314 — Waist.

No. 9302 — Dress sleeves.

No. 9268 — Waist.

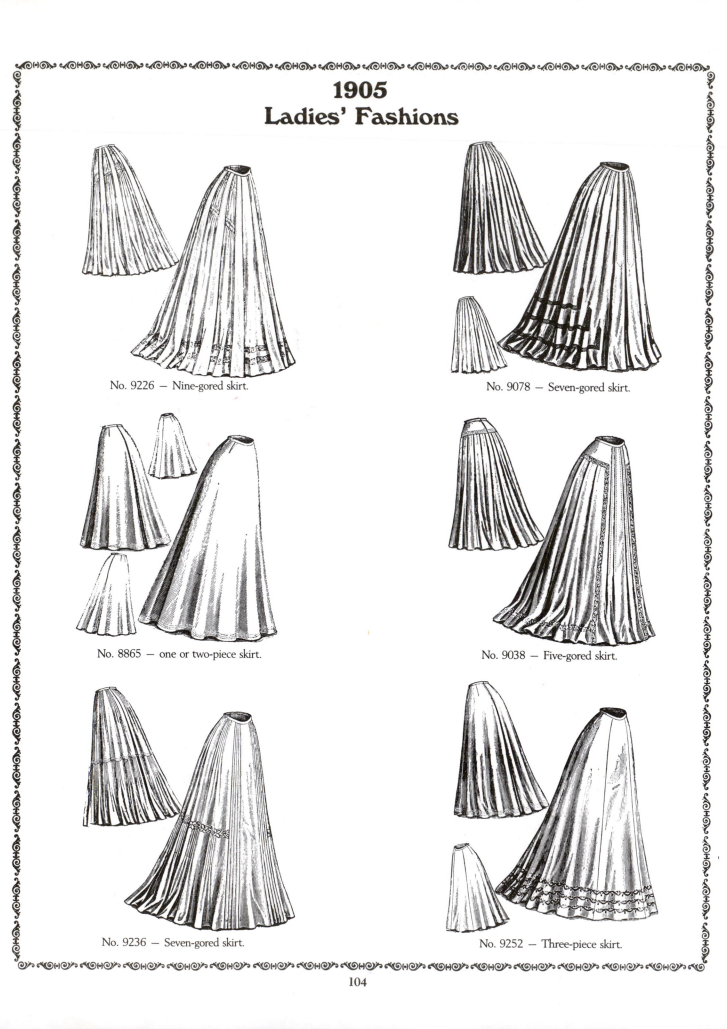

No. 9226 — Nine-gored skirt.

No. 9078 — Seven-gored skirt.

No. 8865 — one or two-piece skirt.

No. 9038 — Five-gored skirt.

No. 9236 — Seven-gored skirt.

No. 9252 — Three-piece skirt.

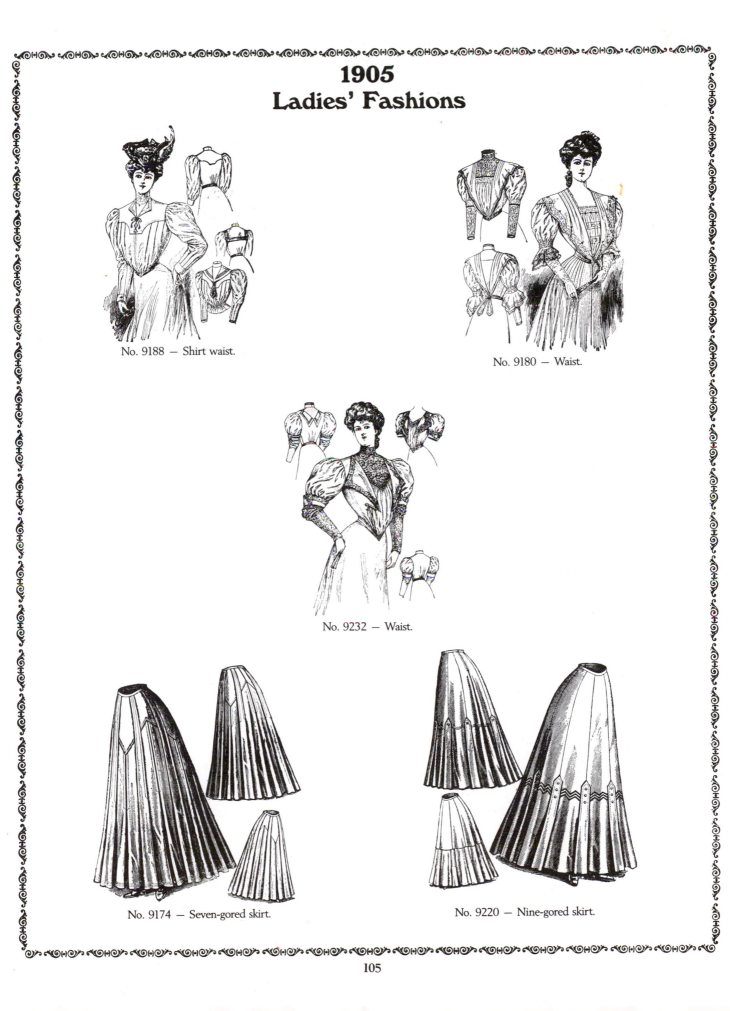

No. 9188 — Shirt waist.

No. 9180 — Waist.

No. 9232 — Waist.

No. 9174 — Seven-gored skirt.

No. 9220 — Nine-gored skirt.

No. 9273 — Henrietta in a bright scarlet shade was used for this attractive little dress. The waist is cut with a box-pleated blouse front below a double-pointed yoke trimmed with fancy black silk braid. The stock is of the material trimmed with this same braid. The closing is formed in the center back which is box-pleated below the yoke in the same manner as the front. The sleeves are very pretty indeed and have double puffs of the material and long fitted cuffs trimmed with the braid, reaching just to the elbow.

The skirt, which is a very jaunty model for a young girl, has five gores and is cut with the yoke and front panel in one piece. It is box-pleated in the sides and back. This frock would also be extremely stylish and pretty if made up of a small, dark blue and green plaid with the yoke and cuffs trimmed wtih dark blue silk gimp and tiny brass buttons.

Five-Gored Skirt

No. 9273

Circular Skirt

No. 9305

No. 9273 — Winter frock.

Five-Gored Skirt

No. 9311

Five-Gored Skirt

No. 9261

No. 9230 — Shirt waist.

No. 9208 — Waist.

No. 9203 — Costume with or without large collar and band flounces.

No. 9193 — Costume suitable for thirteen to seventeen year olds.

No. 9315 — Suitable for six to twleve year olds.

No. 9281 — Suitable for six to twelve year olds.

No. 9277 — Little boys' or girls' pleated apron.

No. 9295 — Suitable for six to twelve year olds.

No. 9307 — Suitable for six to twelve year olds.

1905 Misses' Blouse Waist and Skirt

1905 Girls' Dress

No. 8383 — A square yoke is a noteworthy feature of this little frock. The yoke is seamed on the shoulders and affords support for the full skirt which is regulated by gathers at the top. A standing and a flat collar are given for the high neck, either being suitable, and a French round outline is also provided for and is usually finished with a frill of fine needlework or Valenciennes lace. The full bishop sleeves, which are confined at the wrist by deep cuffs, may be replaced by puff sleeves completed by narrow bands. When made of plain material, the dress may have a hem finished, with or without the trimming ruffle.

This pattern can be developed and worn by girls from six months to ten years of age.

1905
Girls' Costume

No. 8406 — White linen with and without a decoration of hand-embroidery or pale pink lawn trimmed with insertion and edging can be used effectively in this design. Puff sleeves and a Dutch round neck are permissable and a bertha collar of unique shaping is a pretty feature but is not always used. Tucks and gathers are introduced in the full body, the former extending to the waist, and the closing is made at the back. A standing collar is added when the neck is high. Full-length leg-o'-mutton sleeves are supplied with cuffs but may be plainly finished. A deep hem is allowed on the attached skirt which is composed of five gores gathered at the top and has tucks at each side of the front in apparent continuation of those in the body. A belt of the material gives a finish at the waistline.

Pattern No. 8406 is to be worn by girls from three to ten years of age.

1905 Girls' Dress

No. 8370 — A dainty frock is illustrated in dotted swiss with Valenciennes lace, and also in India linon with all-over lace, applique banding and hemstitching. A body lining supports the blousing front and backs which are revealed in square yoke outline and finished in high-necked fashion with a standing band or cut out in French square effect. Full-length bishop sleeves completed by deep cuffs are furnished, as well as those in elbow style shirred to form frills. Five gores were used in constructing the skirt, which is gathered at the top and attached to the lining of the blouse. Trimming ruffles and a fancy bertha decorate the dress prettily, but they may be dispensed with if a plainer effect is desired.

White point d'esprit with a yoke of point de Paris lace and edging for the decoration would make a dainty party frock. Linen would be serviceable if the plain development were employed and lawn, dimity, organdy, mull, etc., will also be suitable for reproducing the mode.

Girls from five to thirteen years old can wear this costume.

1905
Girls' Frocks

No. 9265 — This smart little frock for four to twelve year-old girls is made of red and blue plaid woolen. It is cut with a blouse waist of the material tucked in double box-pleat effect beneath a fancy yoke facing which can, however, be omitted if desired, as shown in one of the smaller views of the medium. The neck is completed by a sailor collar of plain red cloth deeply faced with dark blue velvet. This can be either pointed or square in the front as shown in the different views. The back of the blouse has a yoke facing to correspond with the front (unless it is omitted from the garment entirely) and is laid beneath this in four tucks, the two in the center forming an inverted seam effect. The sleeves are gathered into the shoulders and tucked for a short distance above the narrow cuffs of blue velvet, but if preferred, these tucks can be omitted. The full straight skirt is laid in two tucks on each side of the front and has tucks forming an inverted pleat in the back. It is plainly completed by a deep hem.

No. 9293 — Pale blue albatross with large collar and cuffs of black velvet made this smart little frock which has a long French blouse waist of the material gathered into the neck and decorated just below the chest with two rather deep crossway tucks running straight round the figure. The closing is formed in the center-back. The big collar has a deep point front and back and is decorated with fancy blue silk trimming matching the color of the frock. The stock is of the same material. The sleeves have short, full puffs and long fitted cuffs of the velvet.

Children from two to eight years of age wear this dress suitably.

No. 9265   No. 9293

9265   9293

1905 Children's Fashions

No. 9297 — Child's dress suitable for two to eight year olds.

No. 9317 — Child's apron suitable for two to ten year olds.

No. 9301 — Child's dress suitable for two to eight year olds.

No. 9309 — Child's dress suitable for six months to ten years old.

No. 9263 — Childs' dress suitable for six months to five years old.

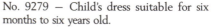

No. 9279 — Child's dress suitable for six months to six years old.

1905 Children's Fashions

No. 9237 — Dress with attached straight gathered skirt suitable for six to twelve year olds.

No. 9229 — Child's dress suitable for three to eight year olds.

No. 9227 — Dress suitable for six to twelve year olds with varied neck, yoke and sleeves.

No. 9207 — Child's dress suitable for one to six year olds.

No. 9215 — Child's empire dress suitable for one to six year olds.

No. 9205 — Dress suitable for six to twelve year olds.

1905 Children's Fashions

No. 9251 — Child's dress suitable for three to eight year olds.

No. 9245 — Child's dress suitable for five to ten year olds.

No. 9239 — Dress.

No. 9225 — Girl's apron.

No. 9233 — Girl's dress with two styles of collar.

1905 Fashions for Dolls

No. 9269 – Girl doll's dress.

No. 9271 – girl doll's coat.

1905 Infants

No. 9313 – Infant's set consisting of cloak (with or without one or two cape collars), Dutch cap and tucked dress (with or without shoulder ruffles).

No. 9209 – Infant's set.

Glossary

People interested in dolls, and consequently in styles and fabrics used in fashions of the late 19th and early 20th centuries, frequently are confronted with words not now part of our vocabulary. We have, therefore, included a list of definitions concerning terms relating to old styles and fashions which are encountered in books and fashion magazines of the period 1880-1905 and some sewing terms, as well as names of various fabrics and styles unique to this period. While the list is not inclusive, it should enable the reader to understand most of the references made in texts from *The Delineator* and other magazines.

Many of the fabrics mentioned in this glossary have been in common use for more than a century, and thus are familiar to us in present-day use, providing a source of fabrics which may be used for authentic costuming of antique dolls.

AIGRETTE: a spray of feathers or gems worn on a hat or in the hair.

ALBATROSS: a lightweight woolen fabric in which the plain weave has been varied to produce a crepe effect. It is usually soft, but has more body than challis.

ALPACA (mohair): a shiny, stiff, wiry cloth made of Angora goat hair and with either cotton, wool or silk filling.

APPLIQUE: the process of cutting out designs of contrasting fabrics and embroidering or sewing them onto a garment for decorative purposes.

ARMSEYE: the opening in a bodice or dress top for inserting a sleeve.

BALBRIGGAN: formerly denoted the highest grade of fine knit underwear, but now applied to any kind of underwear made of Egyptian cotton.

BANDEAU: a band or fillet for the hair.

BASQUE: a woman's blouse made with a tight-fitting waist and with or without a short skirt or peplum attached.

BATISTE: a semi-sheer lightweight cotton fabric with a soft silky feel and a silky appearance, distinguished from nainsook by its finer construction and finish.

BENGALINE: a heavy corded silk fabric with a silk warp and a cotton or worsted filling.

BERTHA: a wide collar worn around a neckline, often made of lace, sometimes of matching or contrasting material.

BOBBINET: see NET.

BOMBAZINE: a fine twilled fabric of silk and worsted or cotton, often dyed black and used for mourning.

BRETELLE: suspender-like shaped bands worn over shoulders and attached in back and front to a waistband; often used to help support a skirt, and sometimes applied as trim.

BUCKRAM: a stiff, coarse, inexpensive cotton cloth heavily sized, used for the linings and frames of hats.

CALICO: an inexpensive cotton fabric with a plain weave and usually a printed pattern. It is rather coarse, heavily sized, and has a slightly glazed finish.

CAMBRIC: a closely woven, rather stiff cotton fabric with a slightly glossy surface. It was often used for underwear, corset-covers, combinations, drawers and chemises.

CAPOTE: A long flowing coat or cloak with a hood, sometimes worn by soldiers, or a very long mantle worn by women. This word is also used to describe a separate full hood.

CASHMERE (cassimere): a soft, lightweight, smooth material in a twill weave, made either of wool or with a cotton or silk warp, and usually found in plain colors. It was used for babies' sacques and coats and children's fall and winter dresses. The name is derived from the source of the wool — the undercoat of a Kashmiri goat.

CHALLIS (cotton): a medium weight cotton fabric finished to resemble wool challis. It usually has a printed pattern and is used when an inexpensive fabric is desired.

CHALLIS (wool): a lightweight woolen fabric in a plain weave or with a small printed design. It was used for dresses and kimonos.

CHAMBRAY: a cotton material, always made with a colored warp and a white filling, which produces a grayed effect. It was often used for children's dresses and rompers, women's dresses and other wear.

CHANTILLY LACE: a delicate lace of silk or linen, having a six-sided mesh ground and a scrolled or floral design.

CHATELAINE: an ornamental hook, clasp or brooch worn at a woman's waist having a chain (or ribbon or string) attached for keys, trinkets, purse, watch or sewing needs.

CHEMISETTE: a vest or dickey, generally sleeveless, made of fine cotton and lace or net; used primarily to fill a low neckline.

CHEVOIT: a strong twilled fabric woven with a colored stripe or cheek.

CHINA SILK: a thin plain silk with a slight luster. It is similar to "Japanese" silk and to "Habutai" and all are used for lining or making baby dresses and ladies' waists.

CLOSURE: opening of any garment which makes it possible to put garment on more easily.

COMBINATION: a top combined with drawers to form a one-piece undergarment. Sometimes referred to as chemise-drawers.

COUTIL: a heavy cotton cloth used for making corsets with herringbone weave and sleek smooth appearance.

CRASH: a term loosely applied to any cotton or linen fabric which is constructed from coarse yarns in a plain loose weave. Better qualities were used for suits, separate skirts and toweling.

CRAVAT: a band or scarf worn around the neck.

CREPE DE CHINE: a fine soft crepe fabric.

CREPON: a fabric resembling crepe but firmer in texture.

CRINOLINE: a coarse, medium weight cotton cloth, heavily sized, more closely woven than buckram and not quite so stiff.

CUIR: French word for leather.

CULOTTE: baby drawers (as opposed to our present use of the word).

CUMMERBUND: a broad pleated sash worn on a dress, usually with a dropped waistline.

DAMASSE SILK: a kind of brocaded silk material.

DIMITY: a very fine, sheer cotton fabric recognized by small cords or groups of small cords arranged in stripes or cross-bars. (Cross-bar dimity is called JACONET.)

DIRECTOIRE: a style of dress prevalent at the time of the French directory, characterized by a great extravagance of design imitating Greek and Roman costumes.

DRAP D'ETE: lightweight cottons suitable for summer wear.

DROPPED FLY: a flap on the front of boys' or men's pants popular up to the 1840s when a standard front fly replaced it for general use.

DUST RUFFLE: a ruffle, usually pleated in pleats from 1/4in (.7cm) to 1in (3cm) of tarlatan edged with lace. This was placed under the hem of children's dresses for stiffening under the skirt, or on floor-length dresses around hemline to "pick up the dust," hence the word "dust ruffle." This also served to hold the skirt out and to stiffen it.

DUVETYN: a soft, short napped fabric with a twill weave, made of cotton, wool, rayon or silk.

ENGLISH NET: See NET.

EPAULETTE: a shoulder ornament.

ETAMINE: a light worsted or cotton fabric with an open mesh.

FAILLE: a ribbed silk fabric recognized by its flat cord surface, the heavy filling cords being not so rounded as those in poplin and grosgrain, and inconspicuous. In effect, faille resembles taffeta, having about the same amount of stiffness.

FICHU: a kind of ornamental three-cornered cape, usually of lace, muslin or silk, worn by women as a covering for the shoulders.

FLOCKING: decorative trim on fabrics consisting of tiny dots either woven in or later applied in the manufacturing process.

FLOUNCE: deep gathered or pleated ruffles.

FLUTER: a small (about 8in [20cm] by 8in [20cm] by 10in [25cm]) pressing machine with two hollow parallel bars indented on the outside with longitudinal ridges that meshed when turned with a handle. These were heated by means of iron rods heated on a stove and inserted into the hollow cores of the brass rollers. Fabrics were run slowly between the rollers and pressed into the long narrow pattern or ridges on the rollers.

FOULARD: a lightweight silk made with a plain twill or satin weave. It has a rich luster on the right side and usually comes in a printed pattern, although it can be bought in plain colors. It feels light, firm, supple and slippery.

FRAISE FASHION: A lacy neck ruffle.

GALLOON: a narrow band or braid used as trimming and commonly made of lace, metallic thread embroidery.

GARIBALDI: A shirtwaist worn by women, so-called from its resemblance in shape to the red shirt worn by Italian patriot Garibaldi, often full and held in at the waistline by a belt.

GARNITURE: decorative trim of all kinds.

GAUGING: See PLEATING, CARTRIDGE.

GEORGETTE: a very thin sheer silk with a crepe finish.

GIMP: an ornamental flat braid or round cord used as trimming.

GINGHAM: a medium weight cotton material which comes in stripes, plaid and plain colors. Finer grades have a higher thread count (number of warp and woof threads used in the weaving process).

GODET: a segment of cloth wider at the bottom than at the top and used as an inset to produce fullness or for widening, such as in a skirt. (Also: Gore.)

GOSSAMER: a type of very sheer fabric.

GRENADINE: a cloth of very open texture constructed in the gauze weave; usually made of silk and worsted. It often has fancy stripes of different weaves.

GROS DE LONDRES: a lightweight silk fabric of about the same texture as taffeta, but having narrow cords alternating with wider ones. The cords are flat and not so apparent as in a poplin or grosgrain. Often the warp and filling are of different colors, giving a changeable effect.

GROSGRAIN: an all-silk fabric with cords that are uniform in size, especially found in ribbon.

GUIMPE: a blouse with either long or short sleeves worn under open-neck dresses.

GUIPURE: a heavy lace with a large pattern.

HABUTAI (wash or tub silk): a lightweight Japanese silk very closely constructed in a plain weave. It has more body, is firmer, heavier and duller than China silk.

HENRIETTA: a fine woolen cloth.

JACONET: (See DIMITY.)

KILT: a small boy's skirted garment sometimes worn over short tight or bloused pants . . . or without. Usually worn by boys from two to five years of age. The word also designates a girl's pleated skirt.

KNICKERS: a development from women's straight leg drawers to a type gathered on a band below the knees with a ruffle of embroidered edging. Boys aged five to fourteen also wore "knickers" from around 1910 to the 1930s (no lace, of course!).

LAMBREQUIN: a scarf worn over a hat to protect against rain, wind and sun.

LAWN: a fine, sheer cotton or linen fabric of plain weave which is thinner than cambric.

LEGHORN: a hat or bonnet made from leghorn straw which is cut green, bleached and plaited, grown in Tuscany, Italy.

LININGS: See BUCKRAM, CRINOLINE, TARLATAN. (Innerlinings for dust ruffles and stiffening.)

LINSEY-WOOLSEY: a wool and linen fabric with linen threads forming the warp and cotton or wool forming the woof or filler.

LISLE: a smooth, tightly twisted thread frequently made of long staple cotton.

LISSE: a kind of smooth gauze used for ruching.

MALINE: See NET.

MANTILLA: a woman's light cloak or cape of silk, velvet, lace or the like, or a kind of veil covering the head and falling down upon the shoulders.

MASALIA: a trade name for a very fine underwear material which is heavier and has more body than nainsook.

MERCERIZING: an important preparatory process for cotton fabrics or linen. Mercerizing causes the flat twisted ribbon-like cotton fiber to swell into a round shape and to contract in length. The fiber becomes much more lustrous and the strength is increased by 20 percent (hence the advantage of mercerized thread for hand- and machine-sewing).

MERINO: a soft lightweight fabric made originally of fine wool. ALSO, a type of fine wool and cotton yarn used for knitting underwear and hosiery.

MESSALINE: a soft, lightweight silk fabric having a satin weave.

MILLINERS WIRE: a type of cotton-wrapped wire packaged in rolls, black and white, and in several weights, used in making ladies' hat frames and children's hats and bonnets.

MOIRE: usually a corded silk or silk-and-cotton fabric with a watered effect produced by pressing.

MONTURE: a few flowers bunched and used for decoration.

MOUSQUETAIRE: various garments emulating the style of French dandies of 17th and 18th centuries, such as gloves with long wide gantlets, sweeping broad-brimmed hats with dashing feathers and fully-trimmed sleeves.

MOUSSELINE DE SOIE (SILK MUSLIN): a thin silk-and-cotton fabric with very little body, often having large printed patterns in soft colors.

MULL: one of the sheerest cotton fabrics made, mercerized with no dressing, hence soft; crushes quickly and needs frequent pressing.

MUSLIN: a term applied to any plain-woven fabric of close construction, ranging from the very finest grades of underwear material to the coarsest sheeting.

NAINSOOK: a thin lightweight cotton with a plain weave and little or no dressing; sometimes mercerized; not so thin and sheer as batiste.

NET:

1. **BOBBINET:** a cotton net, the threads so interwoven that they form octagonal meshes, thus making a thin, transparent but strong fabric.

2. **ENGLISH NET:** a finely meshed fabric made of cotton; the background fabric of many types of lace.

3. **MALINE:** a fine silk or cotton hexagonal mesh netting, heavily sized, especially desirable for veilings and scarves.

4. POINT D'ESPRIT: a fine cotton net with small square spots at close and regular intervals. It is dainty, durable and almost transparent.

5. TULLE: a silk net, very delicate and fragile, used for evening dresses, scarves and trimmings.

NUN'S VAILING: a lightweight wool fabric made with a plain weave in plain colors; similar to wool batiste.

ORGANDY: a sheer, stiff, very lightweight cotton, quite transparent and not durable.

PALETOT: a cloak, usually long, with one or more capes.

PANTALETTE: fancy laced and ruffled legs sewn on a band or elastic and worn from knee to ankle under full skirts.

PASSEMENTERIE: a fancy edging or trimming made of braid, cord, gimp, beading or metallic thread in various combinations.

PEAU DE SOIE: a heavy silk with a fine grainy surface produced by tiny cords, enduring and serviceable.

PELERINE: a full-length cloak or coat, often fur trimmed or fur lined.

PELISSE: a long cloak for outdoor wear, sometimes fur lined.

PERCALE: a cotton fabric with a plain weave, usually recognized by its firm construction, its smooth dull finish and its printed pattern, although it also comes in plain colors.

PERCALINE: a lightweight cotton fabric, usually of one color, with a glossy surface.

PINA CLOTH: a very sheer lustrous cloth with a plain weave made from the fibers of the pineapple. It is strong, durable and attractive, but stiff and unyielding.

PLASTRON: a trimming like a dickey worn on the front of a woman's dress, often of a contrasting fabric narrowing from neck to waist.

PLEATING:

1. BOX PLEATING: a system of pleating two edges together, skipping a space and bringing two more folded edges together.

2. CARTRIDGE PLEATING: a method of pleating great widths of material to be gathered into a small space as, for example, when dressing a china doll with a tiny waist when you want a bouffant skirt. (Also referred to as Organ Pleating or Gauging.)

3. KNIFE PLEATING: ordinary pleats of any size with firmly pressed folds going in the same direction.

4. UNPRESSED PLEATS: pleats sewn in at the top but allowed to hang free with no pressing or crease marks.

PLISSE: a plain weave crepe or crinkled fabric which has been specially treated to maintain the crinkled appearance.

POINT D'ESPRIT: See NET.

POLONAISE: dress top hanging below the waist and often draped in back.

PONGEE: a medium weight silk fabric in plain weave distinguished by its irregular threads. It is made of wild silk, and hence not so regular, fine nor beautiful as fabrics made from cultivated silk.

POPLIN: a fine-ribbed material found in silk, wool, cotton, cotton-and-silk, silk-and-wool and wool-and-cotton. Its warp yarns are so fine and numerous as to cover completely the coarser filling yarns, thus producing fine ribs across the cloth.

RAMIE: a cloth similar to linen, made of ramie fiber which is strong, fine and durable.

RIBBON WIRE: a narrow (1/4in [.7cm] to 1/2in [1cm]) stiff fabric with fine wire molded into each edge.

RUCHE OR RUCHING: a narrow band of net, lace or fine thin fabric, set in pleats or gathers, applied to trim a dress, particularly at necklines and wrists.

SATEEN: a heavy mercerized cotton fabric with a sateen weave, attractive and durable but not so beautiful nor so soft as silk.

SATIN: a lustrous silk material in a satin weave. Satin is always made in the satin or a variation of the satin weave, but it may be finished with either a crepe or a plain back.

SCRIM: a cotton fabric made of heavy yarns in an open plain weave, strong, durable, semitransparent, easily laundered.

SHANTUNG: silk similar to pongee; this is more irregular in weave.

SHIFT: another name for chemise.

SLEEVES:

BISHOP SLEEVE: wide, full sleeve gathered at wrists.

COAT SLEEVE: a straight sleeve with a slight curve at the elbow, or often made in two sections as for suits or tailored garments.

PAGODA SLEEVE: bell-shaped sleeve (about seven-eights length) with sheer gathered undersleeve.

UNDERSLEEVE: sheer partial sleeve, usually quite full, worn under pagoda sleeves...attached on a band to fit over the elbow; gathered at wrists.

SILK BROADCLOTH: a firm lightweight silk fabric with a dull finish distinguished by its characteristic thick and heavy feel without the slipperiness of many silks.

SURAH: a soft but stout silk with a twill weave, usually with a dull surface although satin surah has a rather high luster.

SWISS (muslin): a fine thin cotton fabric rather loosely woven and having a great deal of stiffening. It differs from lawn in being more sheer, more loosely woven and stiffer.

SWISS (dotted): Swiss muslin with dots of heavier yarn at regular intervals. In good grades the dots are woven in and tied so that they will not wash out.

TABLIER: an apron or apron-like part of a woman's dress.

TAFFETA: a plain closely woven, rather stiff silk fabric with a dull luster. Chiffon taffeta is a more soft and pliable fabric. Many taffetas are heavily weighted and do not stand the test of time. (Many grades of taffeta are available in rayon but are usually unsatisfactory because of a bright sheen; they are too stiff to drape well, and do not wear well. They are not recommended for doll clothes.)

TARLATAN: a very loosely constructed cotton cloth, heavily sized, used most extensively for fancy dress costumes and decorative purposes and for ladies' petticoats and dust ruffles.

TORCHON: a type of lace.

TULLE: See NET.

VANDYKES: V-shaped points which form a decorative edging.

VELOUR: a fabric having a velvet-like surface.

VELVET: a pile fabric with the pile usually cut close. Velvets are usually identified further by the kind of backing that is used, thus there are:

1. VELVETEEN with cotton backing and cotton pile.

2. COTTON-BACKED VELVET, a cotton backing with silk pile.

3. SILK-BACKED VELVET with silk pile and silk backing.

4. UPHOLSTERY VELVET with wool, mohair or linen backing.

5. LYONS VELVET with a cotton or silk back and with very close and firm backing.

6. CHIFFON VELVET, an all-silk velvet so woven that the pile is in very narrow stripes so fine that they are not noticeable unless examined closely.

7. PANNE VELVET, a cotton or silk-backed fabric, with pile longer than that of ordinary velvet, pressed to give a smooth, shiny effect.

VICUNA: a fabric made from the fleece of a vicuna (a llama-like animal of the central Andes in South America).

VIGNONE: an all-wool cloth, twilled in neutral colors, originally of Spanish wool.

VOILE: made in cotton, silk and wool, a fabric made of fine, hard-twisted yarns with a plain weave and open mesh.

WARP: threads on a loom used to form the length of the fabric.

WATTEAU: a style of back for a woman's gown in which one or more broad folds are carried from the neck to the floor without being held in at the waist, while the front and sides of the gown are "shaped to the person," providing a sweeping, flowing line in back.

WOOF (also FILLING or WEFT): threads on a loom used to form the width of the fabric.

WORSTED: while woolens and worsteds are both made of wool, there is a difference in the length of the fiber, weave and finish. Woolen yarns have short fibers, tend to be soft and fuzzy. Worsted yarns are longer, tend to be smooth and strong.

ZEPHYR: a fine, lightweight woolen fabric. OR light, fine gingham, thin and silky.

ZIBELINE: a thick lustrous soft fabric of wool and other animal hair such as mohair, having a silky nap.

Pattern

This is a "STAR" dress, or one of our series of dresses copied from original antique doll dresses, as contrasted with our US patterns which are adapted from *The Delineator* fashion magazines of the late 1800s. We refer to this pattern as the RED STAR PATTERN, following the GOLD STAR PATTERN of 1983, and the SILVER STAR PATTERN of 1984 and the BLUE STAR PATTERN in 1987.

General Instructions

1) PLEASE read through the whole pattern before starting to work.
2) Complete all underwear to be worn under dress and place on doll before starting to work so that the dress will fit properly.
3) Cut pattern pieces other than trim of light-weight unbleached muslin or cotton. Assemble following instructions for dress and sleeves. Fit to assure that this pattern is satisfactory for your doll. (See instructions for basic pattern in *Antique Children's Fashions*, page 88).
4) Try cutting skirts in particular crosswise of fabric for softer hanging pleats of folds.

Description of Dress

This costume, sometimes referred to as a Russian-bloused dress, features a long waist, bloused in front over a full skirt which has pleats at center front like those of the bodice. The yoke is made of self-fabric and either left plain or covered with lace, with a wide lace ruffle around both back and front yokes. Full bishop sleeves are fitted at wrists with a narrow band and the neckline is completed with a narrow mandarin-type collar for the larger size, the smaller dress having a bound neckline which may be edged with lace. A sash of ribbon with a large bow completes the trim.

The dress is presented in two sizes, for 28in (71cm) and 16½in (42cm) dolls. Construction details vary slightly, indicated by additional explanations or in some cases by the addition of instructions in parentheses. Please watch for these changes.

Pattern
Note Body Sizes for Dolls

Size 28in (71cm) measures 22½in (57cm) from shoulder to toe.
Size 16½in (42cm) measures 12½in (32cm) from shoulder to toe.

Fabric Requirements

LINING: About 3/4yd (69cm) cotton
DRESS: For size 28in (71cm): 36in (91cm) by 45in (114cm) silk fabric or cotton. For size 16½in (42cm), about 18in (46cm) by 45in (114cm) is required. For reproduction dolls, a variety of polyester fabrics is available.

Cutting Instructions

1. SLIP: Cut of unbleached muslin or suitable cotton, 1 front bodice, 1 front yoke, 2 backs, and 1 skirt measuring 8in (20cm) by 1¾yds (160cm). (For smaller size, the slip pattern has no yoke and the slip skirt measures 3½in (9cm) by 32in (81cm).

2. DRESS: LINING.
   Cut of unbleached muslin or other suitable cotton, 1 front bodice, 1 front bodice yoke, 2 bodice backs, using slip backs, and 1 skirt measuring 6in (15cm) by 1¾yds (160cm). (For size 16½in (42cm) no yoke is used and the skirt lining measures 3½in (9cm) by 32in (81cm). SLEEVES. For 28in (71cm) size, optional lining of very sheer cotton, cut 2.)
   DRESS FABRIC: Cut 1 bodice front, 1 bodice front yoke, 2 bodice backs, 2 bodice back yokes, 2 collars, (for size 16½in (42cm) no collar, but cut bias 1in (2.5cm) by 8in (20cm), 2 sleeves, 2 sleeve bands measuring about 1in (2.5cm) by 4¼in (11cm), (for smaller size no sleeve bands are required), and 1 skirt measuring 8½in (22cm) by 1¾yds (160cm). (For smaller size skirt cut 4½in (12cm) by 32in (81cm), or 3¾in (10cm) by 32in (81cm) for eyelet embroidery.) For larger SKIRT: If eyelet fabric is being used, skirt should measure about 7in (18cm) by 2yds (183cm); no lining required. See CHART OF MEASUREMENTS for review of general measurements.
   LACE: For yoke ruffle size 28in (71cm), edged lace about 2½in (6.4cm) by 1¼yds (112cm), and for size 16½in (42cm), 1½in (3.8cm) by 1yd (91cm).
   (Other trim will vary according to your personal inclinations so no other requirements can be given. Please note, however, that yokes may be lace-covered and narrow lace may be applied to sleeve bands.)

Assembly Instructions

NOTE: Throughout this pattern 3/8in (0.9cm) seam allowances are used for size 28in (71cm) and the usual 1/4in (0.65cm) seam allowance for size 16½in (42cm) as shown on pattern pieces.

SLIP
A1. Machine-stitch gathering stitches on lines shown on front bodice. Matching center fronts of yoke and BODICE, pin at ends and center and machine-stitch. Press up and overcast edge. (Remember, no yoke for size 16½in [42cm]).
A2. SEAMS. Match shoulder seams and side seams of slip front and slip back and machine-stitch. At center back, fold on lines shown to form placket and machine-stitch or stitch by hand.
A3. Place slip on doll, pin placket of BODICE, and check neckline. If it is too large, machine-stitch around neckline on seam line. Pull stitching gently to fit neck. Face neckedge with bias tape. Armseyes may be rolled and stitched by hand or edged with bias.

SKIRT
A4. SKIRT: Fold skirt rectangle, short edges together, and machine-stitch, leaving 2in (5.1cm) free for placket. Press seam open and hem open ends for placket. Machine-stitch 2 rows of gathering stitches along top edge, the first 1/8in (0.31cm) from the edge, the second 3/8in (0.9cm) from the edge. Matching center of skirt with center front of slip BODICE, pin at this point and at the ends of skirt and BODICE. Pull gathering stitches to fit BODICE and machine-stitch between rows of gathering stitches. Press seam upward. Place slip on doll and turn hem to desired length. BASTE in place and do not hem permanently until dress is completed. This will prevent a hemline which may be too long when dress covers the slip.
A5. Sew hooks and threaded loops on slip placket at intervals of about 2in (5.1cm) for size 28in (71cm) and 1½in (3.8cm) for size 16½in (42cm).

DRESS
FRONT BODICE
A6. Using linings cut for dress, assemble as for Slip Top (A1 and A2 only). Put aside.
A7. Working with dress front bodice, pleat as shown on pattern, forming three wide box pleats at center front. (Variation: Use vertical rows of narrow lace in area marked for pleats and gather to fit yoke instead of using pleats).
A8. Front Yoke. Yoke may be trimmed before attaching to BODICE, either by covering

with all-over lace or with any applied lace.

A9. Machine-stitch 2 rows of gathering stitches at top and bottom of BODICE according to pattern. Matching center of top BODICE to center of yoke, right sides together, pull gathering stitches gently to fit yoke and machine-stitch. Flip yoke up and press up gently.

A10. Machine-stitch 2 rows of gathering stitches at top and bottom of back bodice as shown on pattern, match yoke center back and BODICE center back, pull gathering stitches gently in place to fit and machine-stitch.

FRONT BODICE TUCK

A11. Note marks at each side of lower front bodice. Fold solid line to dotted line and tack lightly at side seam. Finger-press this tuck UP. It will remain loose.

SEAMS

A12. Matching shoulder seams of front and back BODICE, and side seams, machine-stitch and press open. Staystitch around neckline on seam line.

COMBINING LINING AND DRESS BODICES

A13. Slide dress bodice over lining, with seams inside. Tack at shoulder seams, blind-stitch at yoke seams and around armseyes. Matching lining and BODICE at the bottom, tack at bottom of side seams. Pull gathering stitches gently to fit around bottom and baste in place. (NOTE: Optional method may be used after skirt is completed. Matching skirt center front and BODICE center front, and center backs, right sides together, machine-stitch all around. With seam facing upward, bring lining to machine-stitched line, turn under 1/4in (0.65cm) and hand-stitch in place, thus hiding seam. THEN flip dress over lining and tack as previously indicated.) (Note: Dress top is longer than lining at both back and front which gives the desired bloused effect.)

FITTING BODICE

A14. Using fold lines on BODICE center back as marked on pattern, baste as shown, treating dress lining and dress fabric as one. This is a tentative line which may be altered when BODICE is fitted. Place BODICE on doll over all underwear to be worn; pin at center back to determine whether the fit is correct. Check neckline in particular. If it appears to be a little loose, pull staystitches gently to achieve a perfect fit. It may be necessary to clip to stitch line to check this accurately. When you are satisfied that BODICE is fitted properly, remove and hand-stitch placket in place. Sew hooks and threaded loops down center back, starting 2in (5.1cm) below neckline, and stopping 2in (5.1cm) above BODICE bottom. Top and bottom

fastenings will be added after neckline is finished and skirt has been added. For size 16½in (42cm), hooks should be placed 1½in (3.8cm) apart.

SLEEVES for size 28in (71cm)

A15. Machine-stitch 2 rows of gathering stitches at top and bottom edge of sleeve as shown on pattern. Matching side seams of sleeve, right side inside, stitch sleeve seam from top to mark at wrist edge where placket will be formed. Press seam open all the way to wrist edge, turn once more at opening and hand-stitch to form placket.

SLEEVE BANDS for size 28in (71cm)

A16a. Using bands cut of dress fabric, match ends of bands to ends of sleeve bottom and at center, allowing 1/4in (0.65cm) seam allowance at each end. Pull gathering stitches gently to fit, pin in place and machine-stitch. Turn band to inside, fold seam allowance over and turn loose edge 1/4in (0.65cm). Place this edge on row of machine-stitching and hand-stitch in place. Sew hook on end of band and a threaded loop on band to achieve a firm fit around wrist.

SLEEVES for size 16½in (42cm)

A16b. Sleeve hem. On each side of sleeve seam for 1½in (3.8cm) turn 1/8in (0.31cm) fold and baste, for placket. At wrist edge fold 1/2in (1.3cm) and press, blind-stitching at ends. Machine-stitch 2 rows of gathering stitches positioned as shown on pattern. Pull stitches to fit wrist, distribute gathers evenly, and hold securely in place by backing with a bit of tape tacked over gathers. Hand-stitch hook and threaded loop for closure.

SETTING SLEEVES for both sizes

A17. Matching sleeve underarm with bodice underarm, distribute gathers in yoke area with right sides together and pull gathering stitches to fit armseye. (NOTE: There are no gathers for about 1½in (3.8cm) on either side of underarm seam.) Place bodice on doll over all underwear to be worn and check sleeve for correct fit. When satisfied with sleeve fit, either machine-stitch or hand-stitch in place.

COLLAR

A18. Place bodice on doll and check fit of neckline as for neckline of slip before sewing on collar. COLLAR. For size 28in (71cm) place collar of dress fabric and lining together, right sides inside, and machine-stitch the top or curved edge of collar. Turn right sides out and press. Turn seam allowance of collar 1/4in (0.65cm) and press. Mark center front of collar and pin to center front of neckline. Then pin carefully at intervals around neckline to center back, allowing 1/4in (0.65cm) seam allowance to extend be-

yond placket. Blindstitch collar in place; turn in seam allowances at each end and along edges of collar lining. Pin lining in place and blindstitch in place. (The collar could be applied differently but it is so small that this is actually much easier.) For size 16½in (42cm) dress, use bias to bind neckline.

DRESS SKIRT

A19. Using the two rectangles for the skirt lining and dress fabric, place two long edges right sides together and machine-stitch. Press seam toward lining. Place short ends of skirt together and machine-stitch, leaving 2½in (6.4cm) (1½in [3.8cm] for size 16½in [42cm] at each end free.)

These will form skirt placket.

PLEATING SKIRT.

A20. Bring long edges of rectangles together and baste, pressing hem lightly. Using markings on pattern, form three box pleats at center front, press lightly and baste in place. (VARIATION: Skirt may be gathered instead of having center pleats.) Turn unsewn short ends on seam allowance and hand-stitch so that both ends are closed. Machine-stitch two rows of gathering stitches across top of skirt starting from each end of pleated area and continuing to center back, stopping short 1/2in (1.3cm) from placket.

GATHERING SKIRT

A21. Matching center front of BODICE with center front of skirt, right sides together and pleats matching, baste pleated areas. Match center back of BODICE and center back of skirt and pull gathering stitches to fit. Distribute gathers evenly and baste to BODICE. Machine-stitch. Attach hook and threaded loop to complete the placket.

YOKE TRIM

A22. RUFFLE AROUND NECK. Using a piece of lace 2½in (6.4cm) by 36in (91cm), machine-stitch 2 rows of gathering stitches on straight edge, mark center of lace and place at center front, ends at center backs. Distribute gathers evenly and hand-stitch in place. Small flowers may be placed in yoke corners and/or narrow knotted ribbon may be tacked lightly over gathering line.

Variations

Many variations are possible in making this dress, not only the simple and obvious means of changing color, fabrics and types of trim, but the box-pleated style shown in our pictures may be altered to allow for a simple gathered bodice with gathered skirt to match. If a gathered bodice is desired, less fabric will be required. Please note on pattern a dotted line which indicates the fold line for cutting this style, and the picture of the eyelet dress. The skirt may be cut as shown, but in the assembly of the skirt, eliminate the pleats.

The bodice, including yoke, may be covered with sheer English net and basted lightly to pattern pieces before starting assembly or the yoke may be trimmed with rows of narrow lace gathered slightly. The neck ruffle, which is shown here in lace, might be made of self-fabric and edged with lace. On the bodice before pleating, the exposed part of each pleat may be covered with lace (insertion may be used here) and the edges of the lace may be feather-stitched or otherwise highlighted. Refer to the picture of the smaller doll to see the result of this trim. Only the limits of your imagination will bring an end to the ways in which this pattern may be varied. We hope you will enjoy using this pattern many times. Good luck!

CHART FOR MEASUREMENTS OF VARIOUS PATTERN REQUIREMENTS

	Size 16½in (42cm)	Size 28in (71cm)
Skirt fabric	4½in (12cm) by 32in (81cm)	8½in (22cm) by 1¾in (4.5cm)
Eyelet fabric	3½in (9cm) by 32in (81cm)	7in (18cm) by 2yd (183cm)
Skirt lining	3½in (9cm) by 32in (81cm)	6in by 1¾yds
Neck ruffle lace	1½in (3.8cm) by 1yd (91cm)	2½in (6.4cm) by 1¼in (3.2cm)
Dress ribbon	1½in (3.8cm) by 1¼yd (112cm)	3in (7.6cm) by 1¼yd (112cm)
Width of dress bow, finished	4½in (12cm)	8in (20cm)

Hat

This delightful hat, designed for a 28in (71cm) doll with a head circumference of about 16in (41cm), is constructed with a wire frame over which is placed two ruffles on the brim, and a crown which may be made in one of the two versions offered, Version A being constructed with a crown made of a 11½in (29cm) circle of fabric, the other of a long rectangular piece of dress fabric. The doll milliner may want to experiment before deciding which of the two she prefers. For the 16½in (42cm) doll, a dress pattern is indicated in this fold-out pattern. No hat is given, but two hats fitting this doll may be found in *Costume Cameos 3* by Hazel Ulseth and Helen Shannon.

MATERIALS REQUIRED:

For the WIRED FRAME:
1. Muslin, 1 length 6½in (17cm) by 21in (53cm)
2. Muslin, 1 length 3in (7.6cm) by 36in (91cm)
3. Milliners wire #21.
   a. 14in (36cm) plus 1in (2.5cm) at each end, or a total of 16in (41cm).
   b. 16in (41cm) plus 1in (2.5cm) at each end, or a total of 18in (46cm).
   c. 21in (53cm) plus 1in (2.5cm) at each end, or a total of 23in (58cm).

Materials required for the HAT, consisting of 2 ruffles of hat fabric, 1 crown and 1 hat button.
1. CROWN:
   a. Version A. Of hat fabric 1 circle measuring 11½in (29cm) in diameter and 1 circle the same size of soft cotton.
   b. Version B. Of hat fabric 1 rectangle measuring 4¼in (11cm) by 36in (91cm) (for sheer fabric, soft cotton lining to match).
2. HAT RUFFLES:
   a. Cut of hat fabric 1 rectangle measuring 2¾in (7.1cm) by 30in (76cm).
   b. Cut of hat fabric 1 rectangle measuring 3in (7.6cm) by 36in (91cm).
3. HAT BUTTON:
   a. Cut 1 circle of cardboard measuring 1½in (3.8cm).
   b. Cut of muslin 2-3in (7.6cm) circles of muslin and 2-3in (7.6cm) circles of hat fabric.

Assembly of Wired Frame

CROWN
1. Using muslin measuring 6½in (16cm) by 21in (53cm), mark according to the pattern shown in *Illustration No. 1* and hand-stitch 1 row of large gathering stitches (1¾in from top). Next, fold on line shown at center of pattern and machine-stitch 3/16in (0.45cm) from fold to form a casing for the 14in (36cm) wire. At the bottom, fold on line shown and stitch 3/16in (0.45cm) from fold to form a casing for the 16in (41cm) wire. See Illustration No. 2.

INSERTING WIRE IN CASING
(HINT: To ease inserting wire in casing, use pliers to turn one end of wire over about 1/8in (0.31cm) and flatten. After inserting wire, snip off this turned end.)
2. Insert 14in (36cm) wire in casing indicated, distributing gathers evenly around wire, and secure wire ends by overlapping at 1in (2.5cm) marks and wrap with thread, using a touch of glue.
3. Repeat for 16in (41cm) wire which should be inserted in the bottom casing and repeat as above to secure. Again distribute gathers evenly along wire.
4. Bring short ends of rectangle together and hand-stitch neatly. It may be necessary to release a few stitches to overlap the edges of the rectangle before sewing, and one edge of the rectangle should be turned under 1/8in (0.31cm) before sewing.
5. Pull gathering stitches at top as tight as possible and tie thread to secure gathers. The excess fabric at the top, above the gathers, will be folded over and basted in place to provide a little bulk. See Illustration No. 3.

Brim of Frame

6. Using the 3in (7.6cm) by 36in (91cm) muslin, fold lengthwise and press. Taper at cut edges to a width of about 2½in (6.4cm) as shown in *Illustration No. 4*. Baste, cut edges together and machine-stitch 2 rows of gathering stitches along cut edges 1/8in (0.31cm) from edge and 1/4in (0.65cm) from edge to provide gathering where brim is attached to crown.
7. On folded edge, machine-stitch 2 rows of stitches to form a casing for the 21in (53cm) wire, the first stitching 1/4in (0.65cm) from fold, the second 1/2in (1.3cm) from fold. Insert 21in (53cm) wire using same technique as that described in ;2, lapping and securing as before.

Completing Frame

8. Using small safety pins as markers, divide CROWN into 4 equal parts and mark with safety pins. Repeat for BRIM.
9. Pull gathering stitches along cut edge to fit CROWN, distributing gathers evenly. Matching center backs and center fronts and remaining marker pins, place BRIM on OUTSIDE of frame over the wire and hand-stitch brim to crown.

THIS COMPLETES THE WIRED FRAME...so on to the next step, which is more fun!

Assembling Top of Hat

RUFFLES OF BRIM
10. Using fabric measuring 2¾in (7.1cm) by 36in (91cm), face one long edge with 5/8in (1.6cm) lace (even insertion will work nicely), by placing wrong side of lace on wrong side of hat fabric, with sewing edge of lace extending 1/8in (0.31cm) beyond edge of fabric, and hand or machine-stitch in place 1/4in (0.65cm) from edge of fabric. Flip lace over and outward; fold fabric on the stitching, allowing LACE to extend over fabric about 1/2in (1.3cm). Press in place and stitch. This serves to face fabric edge.
11. Machine-stitch 2 rows of gathering stitches along the other long edge of ruffle. Seam short ends (center back) and once again mark edge in quarter-sections with small safety pins.
12. Pull gathering stitches to fit hat wire (16in [41cm]) of frame. Distribute gathers evenly and set ruffle in place matching center front and center backs, and sides. Position this ruffle so that lace edge will extend about 5/8in (1.6cm) over frame. Note that gathering stitches will be well above the 16in (41cm) wire. Hand-stitch in place. Treat the second ruffle (3in [7.6cm] by 36in [91cm]) in exactly the same way and place over the first ruffle, allowing it to extend about 1/4in (0.65cm) beyond the first.

BUTTON FOR CROWN
13. Using cardboard circle, pad with 2 layers of muslin, folding muslin over sides and gluing in place. Cover them with the hat fabric. (Small running stitches may be sewn around the edge of the hat fabric, button may be placed on circle and stitches pulled to fit around button.)

CROWN
14. Version A: Circle Crown. Using circle of hat fabric and lining, place hat fabric on lining right side. From the center cut a 3in (7.6cm) circle.
Machine-stitch lining and hat fabric together, turn right side out and press seam. Baste around the center opening. Hand-stitch 1 row of 1/8in (0.31cm) gathering stitches on both inside and the outside edge. FOR BUTTON. Pull stitching on inner circle to a size somewhat smaller than the hat button which is to fit over this opening. Distribute gathers evenly and sew hat button in place with blindstitch.

15. Mark outer circle in quarters and pull gathering stitches to fit frame around 16in (41cm) wire, distributing gathers evenly. Set crown over frame so that edge comes below stitching on ruffle, matching quarter markings with those on frame and hand-stitch. And *VOILA!* You are almost finished.

OR

16. Version B. Alternate crown. This version differs from the former only in the use of a rectangle instead of a circle. (If hat fabric is very sheer, line with soft cotton). Place lining over hat fabric and baste all around. Machine-stitch short ends together. Machine-stitch 2 rows of gathering stitches along both long edges of rectangles. (For a really elegant look, use cartridge pleating for the edge on which button will be placed). Either cartridge-pleat to hat button or pull gathering stitches to fit button as in Version A and blindstitch button.

17. Mark lower edge in quarters, pull gathering stitches to fit frame and proceed as in Version A.
AND YOU HAVE ACHIEVED THE MIRACLE OF A LOVELY FLOPPY BONNET. So, on to trim.

18. BONNET TRIM. Using ribbon either 1/2in (1.3cm) or 5/8in (1.6cm) in width, knot loosely at even intervals (about every 2½in [6.4cm]), lay over gathered edge of crown, and tack in place, covering edge of crown. A small bow may be placed at center back.

19. LITTLE BONUS because you have worked so hard! A rosette...to be used for hat trim or perhaps on the yoke of the larger dress.
Using a 1½yd (137cm) piece of ¼in (0.65cm) ribbon, cut as follows:
    8 pieces 1¾in (4.5cm) long, 1st row
    8 pieces 1¾in (4.5cm) long, 2nd row
    4 pieces 1¾in (4.5cm) long, 3rd row
    4 pieces 1¾in (4.5cm) long, 4th row
    2 pieces 1½in (3.8cm) long, 5th row
    2 pieces 1½in (3.8cm) long, 6th row
    1 piece 1¼in (3.2cm) long, center
Cut 2 circles of muslin 3/4in (2cm) in diameter and glue (we use white glue) together to form a base. To form this lovely rosette: Starting with the first 8 ribbons, position them evenly around the muslin base, as shown in *Illustration No. 1*, gluing into place, wrong sides up. Then glue loose ends in place to form loop, as shown in *Illustration No. 2*. Position the next 8 ribbons evenly between the first 8 loops and slightly nearer the center of the base, following the same procedure. Repeat with the next four ribbons, in the third row, and continue with Rows 4, 5 and 6, distributing loops to fill in spaces evenly. The last piece of ribbon may be glued to form a loop and placed in the center of the rosette.

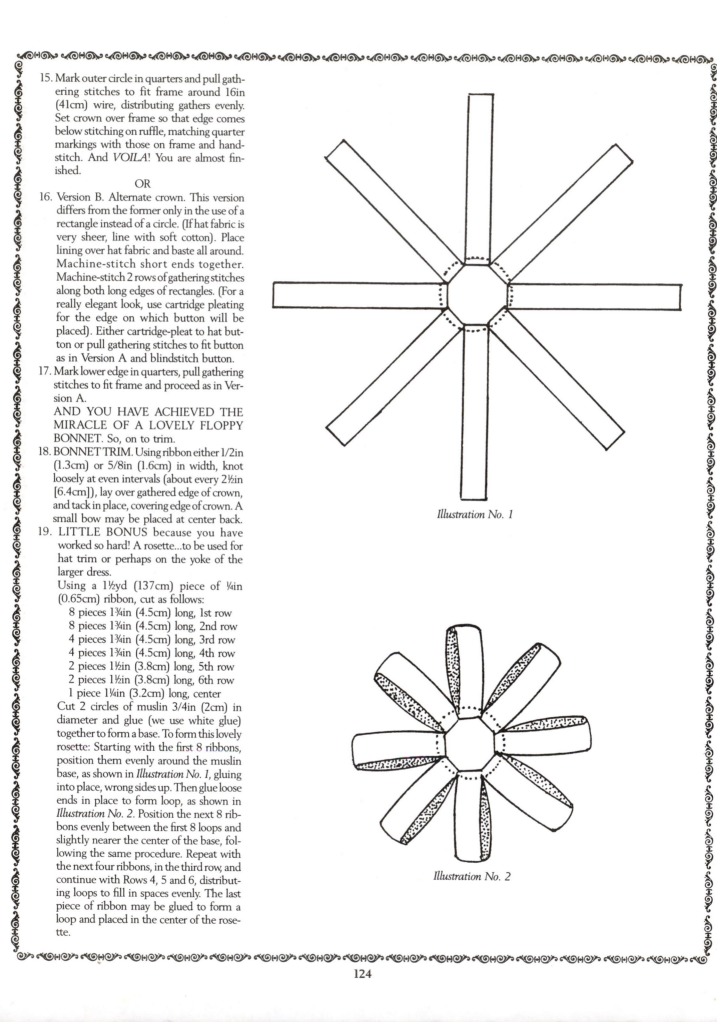

Illustration No. 1

Illustration No. 2

Illustration No. 1
(to scale)
showing construction of crown
for hat for 28in (71cm) doll.

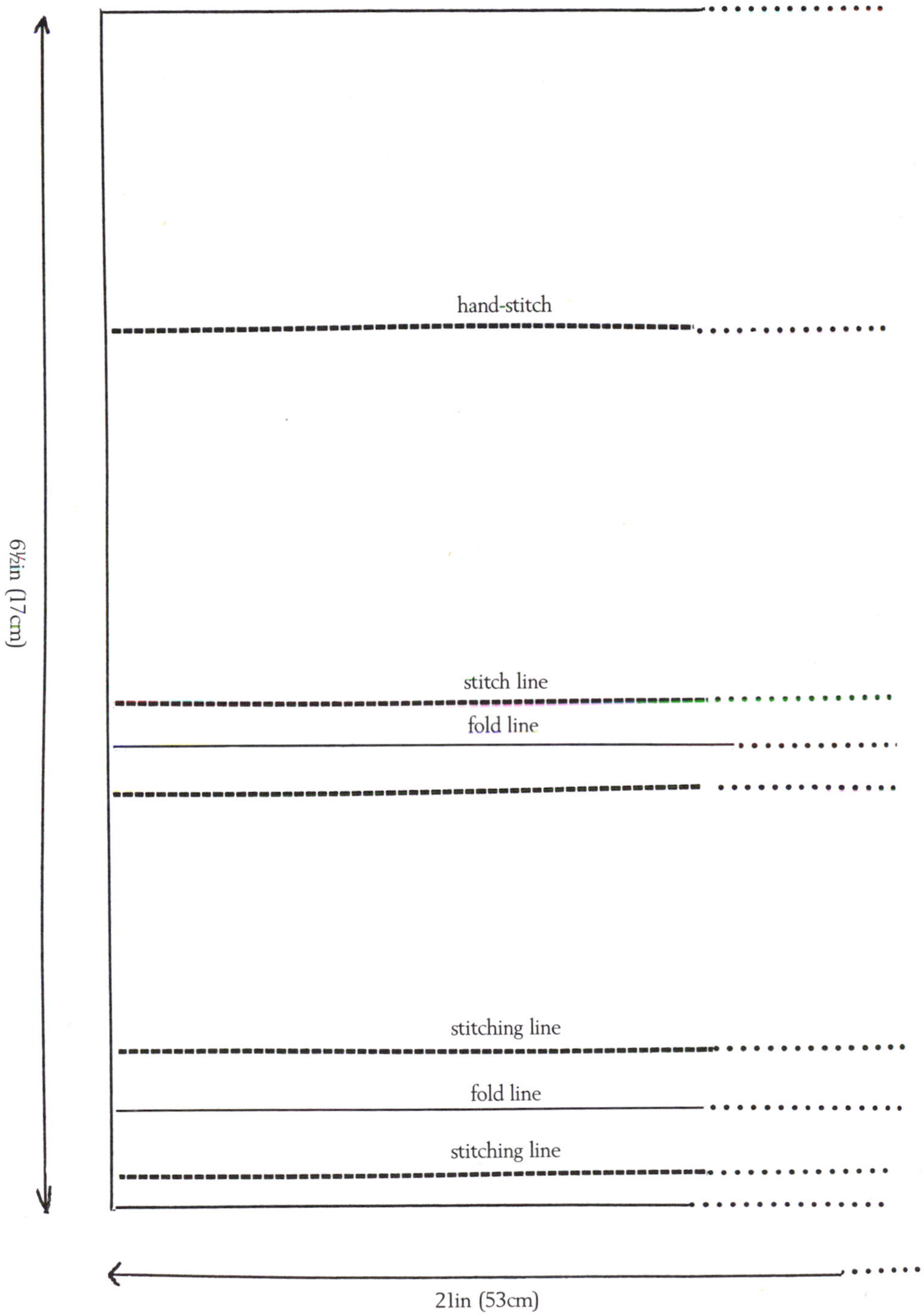

hand-stitch

stitch line

fold line

stitching line

fold line

stitching line

6½in (17cm)

21in (53cm)

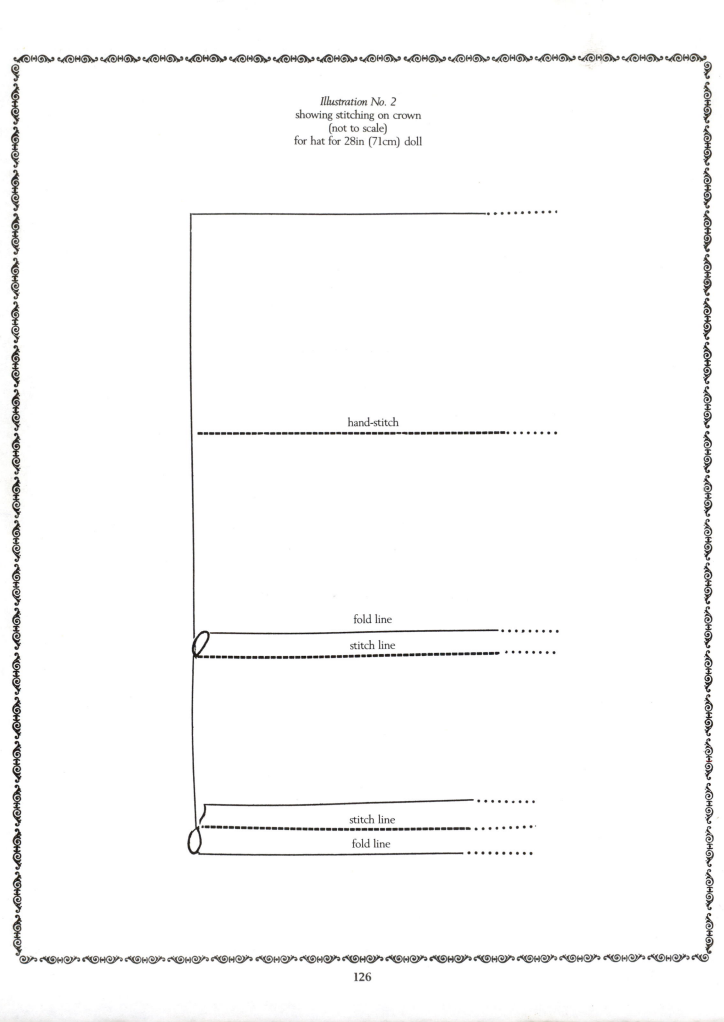

Illustration No. 2
showing stitching on crown
(not to scale)
for hat for 28in (71cm) doll

hand-stitch

fold line

stitch line

stitch line

fold line

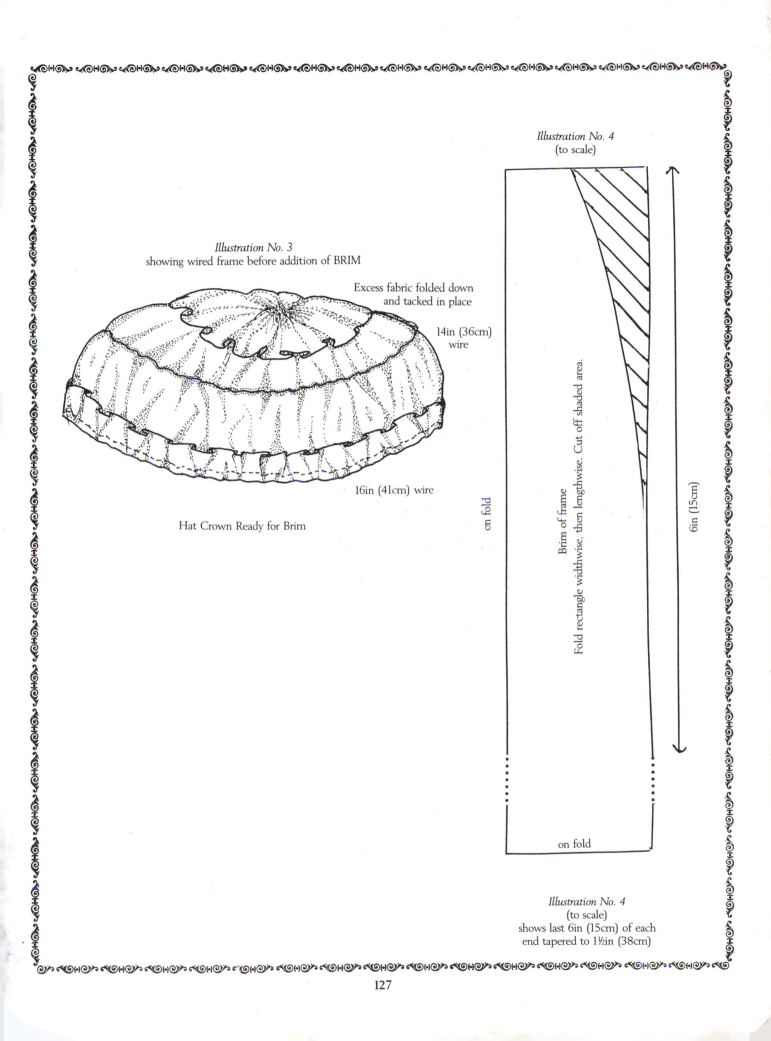

Illustration No. 3
showing wired frame before addition of BRIM

Excess fabric folded down
and tacked in place

14in (36cm)
wire

16in (41cm) wire

Hat Crown Ready for Brim

Illustration No. 4
(to scale)

on fold

Brim of frame
Fold rectangle widthwise, then lengthwise. Cut off shaded area.

6in (15cm)

on fold

Illustration No. 4
(to scale)
shows last 6in (15cm) of each
end tapered to 1½in (38cm)

About the Authors

Hazel Ulseth and Helen Shannon have written several doll dressmaking resource books over a number of years. Among their most popular are *Costume Cameos 1* through *5, Antique Children's Fashions 1880-1890. A Handbook for Doll Costumers, Creating Fur Teddy Bears: Mink and Fake Fur* and *Victorian Fashions Volume I — 1880-1890*. Both *Victorian Fashions Volumes I* and *II* are filled with period dresses and suggestions for making them both for adults and children. Ulseth and Shannon have contributed many doll and teddy bear costume and making projects to *Doll Reader*s and *Teddy Bear and friends*s magazines. They frequently give workshops on doll costuming and teddy bear making at large toy and doll shows throughout the country.

Hazel Ulseth   Helen Shannon